Darrell,
Merry Christmas 198[...]
lots of love
Syd, Gillian, Bill & Kelly
xx

MARILYN MONROE

MARILYN MONROE

AN APPRECIATION BY EVE ARNOLD

ALFRED A. KNOPF, NEW YORK, 1987

ALSO BY EVE ARNOLD

THE UNRETOUCHED WOMAN
FLASHBACK! THE 50'S
IN CHINA
IN AMERICA

THIS IS A BORZOI BOOK PUBLISHED BY ALFRED A. KNOPF, INC.
TEXT COPYRIGHT © 1987 BY EVE ARNOLD
PHOTOGRAPHS COPYRIGHT © 1987 BY EVE ARNOLD
ALL RIGHTS RESERVED UNDER INTERNATIONAL AND PAN-AMERICAN
COPYRIGHT CONVENTIONS. PUBLISHED IN THE UNITED STATES
BY ALFRED A. KNOPF, INC., NEW YORK, AND SIMULTANEOUSLY
IN CANADA BY RANDOM HOUSE OF CANADA LIMITED, TORONTO.
DISTRIBUTED BY RANDOM HOUSE, INC., NEW YORK.
LIBRARY OF CONGRESS CATALOGING-IN-PUBLICATION DATA
ARNOLD, EVE, [DATE]
MARILYN — AN APPRECIATION.
1. MONROE, MARILYN, 1926-1962. 2. MOVING-PICTURE
ACTORS AND ACTRESSES — UNITED STATES — BIOGRAPHY.
I. TITLE.
PN2287.M69A74 1987   791.43'028'0924 [B]   86-46145
ISBN 0-394-55672-0
MANUFACTURED IN THE UNITED STATES OF AMERICA
FIRST EDITION

THIS BOOK IS FOR ED

MARILYN MONROE

n the early 1950's, Marilyn Monroe saw an article of mine in *Esquire* which she liked. She asked a colleague to introduce us. The pictures were of a recording session in which Marlene Dietrich sang "Lili Marlene" and other songs she had made famous during the war. The piece had received attention because it was documentation, a departure from the carefully lit, posed and retouched genre of movie-star studio portraits. Since Dietrich was known to be extremely knowl-edgeable about, and a stickler for, proper lighting and camera work, it was con-sidered both a coup and an innovation to have been permitted to photograph her on a bare, neon-lit soundstage while she was at work.

When we met at a party at "21" given for John Huston, Marilyn asked—with that mixture of naïveté and self-promotion that was uniquely hers—"If you could do that well with Marlene, can you imagine what you can do with *me*?" I smiled and said I would be delighted to try and that I would talk to my editor at *Esquire*.

So began a professional friendship which was helpful to us both. She adored posing for the still camera, and her way of getting to stardom—and stay-ing there—was to stay in the public eye. What better way than a picture story, which filled more column inches than text possibly could? Remember that this was the heyday of the picture magazine—pre-television.

For me she was a joy to photograph, and as her fame increased she became a source of many magazine pages, and having access to her earned me a certain cachet in editors' eyes.

By the time we did the first pictures, she had checked out the fact that I was a member of the prestigious photographers' cooperative Magnum Photos, which had offices in New York and Paris and agents who distributed our work worldwide. Because I owned the copyright, a story done for *Esquire* meant distribution abroad. She loved the idea of one photography session yielding multiple venues.

Our *quid pro quo* relationship, based on mutual advantage, developed into a friendship. The bond between us was photography. She liked my pictures and was canny enough to realize that they were a fresh approach for present-ing her—a looser, more intimate look than the posed studio portraits she was used to in Hollywood.

At this time she was a starlet and still relatively unknown. She had just appeared in a small part in *The Asphalt Jungle*, in which she was transcendent. She was on her way up and anxious for all the press help she could garner, and she expected my pictures to get space for her in newspapers and magazines. Over the years I found myself in the privileged position of photographing someone who I had first thought had a gift for the still camera and who turned out to have a genius for it.

Although she seemed prodigal with what she offered when we worked together and was gracious when we met, socially she always seemed to withhold something of herself, as though by giving too much away she might be misunderstood. It was hard to gauge what was beneath the surface. That kept me guessing as to how much more there was to her that she kept hidden from the camera, and it kept my interest high in her as a subject.

I photographed her six times during the decade that I knew her. The shortest session was two hours and the longest was two months, when I saw her daily during the making of the film *The Misfits*.

When she died, I had thousands of photographs of her. I embargoed all but the few that were in the files of the Magnum offices and those of our agents. I didn't want to exploit the material. Because we had had the unique but complicated relationship that sometimes exists between photographer and subject, she stayed on the screen of my mind. Often when assigned to take pictures of a personality or a head of state, I couldn't help making comparisons. I never knew anyone who even came close to Marilyn in natural ability to use both photographer and still camera. She was special in this, and for me there has been no one like her before or after. She has remained the measuring rod by which I have—unconsciously—judged other subjects.

Twenty-five years after her death, I am still haunted by her as she appeared before my lens. In this book I go back to pictures of her to try to understand why. By seeing her through photographs—the only way most people ever saw her—it may be possible to get some idea of how she saw herself and perhaps to glean some insight into the phenomenon that was Marilyn Monroe.

There is yet another reason for this book. One day Marilyn spoke to me of the Dietrich story that had brought us together. The headline read: "Marlene… an Appreciation." Suddenly she was shy and stammered: "Do you think someday you could do an appreciation of me?"

Yes, Marilyn. Here it is.

P hotographs are not made in a vacuum. The person before the lens is inseparable from the process. To assess the photographs, it helps to know something about the subject. Perhaps hindsight may help to bring clarity.

In the '50's and early '60's I did not analyze Marilyn, but after she died so much was attributed to her—she was eulogized and vilified, exploited and stigmatized (and, as someone said, she could not even have equal time to answer back)—that I started to examine her. But only in the way in which I knew her best. That is, her passion and pursuit of the still camera.

I want to follow her not into her illness or her death, or even into areas of her life I could have no knowledge of, but into the areas which affected the way she saw and created herself and which were expressed in her personality and are thus evident in photographs of her.

We think we know about her life, but perhaps it would be a good idea to refresh our memories. Her sensuality and uninhibited freshness captured the world's imagination. She lived an amazing life (and died a mysterious death —at thirty-six) that reads like a fairy tale fashioned by publicists and promoters. Much of it was—but with help from the lady herself. She brought forth her own blend of diligence, concentration and singlemindedness to achieve what she did.

Cartier-Bresson, the master photographer, called her an American phenomenon. Perhaps only America could have produced her, and only in that zippered but louche time, the 1950's.

She started her career by modeling, went from that to movie extra, to bit player, to starlet, to star and, with her death, to megastar.

In one month, she was on the cover of thirteen magazines (if one can believe her publicists); she was the first centerfold of *Playboy*; she was on the cover of *Life* four times, the cover of *Time* twice. Her fan mail exceeded that of all other Hollywood actresses of her years put together. She really worked at promoting herself.

Louella Parsons named her Movie Glamour Girl. She received the *Redbook* Magazine Award for Best New Screen Personality; the Italian Oscar—the David di Donatello; the French Oscar—the Crystal Star; a New York Film Critics' nomination; an award as Favorite Actress of the World Theatre Owners and Distributors. She never received the coveted American Oscar even though her grosses showed that she could pack in the public at the movie houses, and *Some Like It Hot* became one of the most profitable films ever made.

She appeared in films with some of the top actors of the period: Clark Gable, Bette Davis, Lionel Barrymore, Barbara Stanwyck, Jack Lemmon, Tony Curtis, Claudette Colbert, Cary Grant, Charles Laughton, Jane Russell, Lauren Bacall, Betty Grable, Robert Mitchum, Laurence Olivier, Montgomery Clift and the Marx Brothers.

She was directed by some of the best directors in the world: John Huston, Joshua Logan and Billy Wilder.

She was photographed by the most gifted photographers of her time: Henri Cartier-Bresson, Inge Morath, Richard Avedon, Philippe Halsman, Cecil Beaton, Bruce Davidson, Milton Greene, Bert Stern, Ernst Haas, Elliott Erwitt, Cornell Capa, Dennis Stock, Erich Hartmann and Burt Glinn.

She rode a pink elephant in the circus, appeared on national television with Ed Murrow, was immortalized in wax in Madame Tussaud's in London, went on radio with Edgar Bergen and his dummy Charlie McCarthy, received a Cadillac as a gift from Jack Benny for a radio appearance she made with him, and her footprints and hand prints were impressed in wet cement at Grauman's Chinese Theatre in Los Angeles. For one day the town of Monroe, New York, was renamed Marilyn Monroe, New York; in New York City her image with skirt blowing above her thighs to publicize the film *The Seven Year Itch* was blown up on a billboard four stories high; she was grand marshal of the Miss America contest in Atlantic City, where she posed with each of the forty-eight contestants.

During her lifetime and after her death there were (and still are) look-alike Marilyn strippers, look-alike Marilyn female impersonators, look-alike Marilyn transvestites, look-alike Marilyn contests and Marilyn look-alikes who can be hired for a party.

There are millions of dollars' worth of artifacts of Marilyn Monroe currently on the market worldwide: purses, dolls (one sells for $6,000), penknives, spoons, dresses, stamp pads, posters, greeting cards. When she died, the Strasbergs inherited the bulk of her estate. When Paula Strasberg died, her husband remarried and after Lee's death his widow, Anna Strasberg, took over and franchised the licensing of Monroe objects through her lawyer.

The nude calendar (incidentally, there were only two pictures—a vertical and a horizontal) has sold in the millions, more than any other pin-up (to use a '50's word) before or since.

After her death, painters and illustrators moved in on photographs of her and converted them into icons of sorts. There was Warhol and his silk-screen over-painting on existing photographs. Of it he has said, "It was all so simple —quick and chancy. I was thrilled by it. My first experiment with screens were heads of Troy Donahue and Warren Beatty, and when Marilyn happened to die that month, I got the idea to make screens of her beautiful face—the first Marilyn."

Willem de Kooning made some lively paintings of women of which Marilyn was the inspiration. He has said of them, "They seem vociferous and ferocious. I think it had to do with the idea of the idol, the oracle and, above all, the hilariousness of it."

There was to follow a far less exalted group—a whole school of studio illustrators who made their own brand of studio "art."

It was open season on the photographers who had taken pictures of her. Their photographs were printed without a by-your-leave. No part of her was left unexposed. Old studio pictures were all commandeered. The results ranged from crude to vulgar. One of the most provocative was called "Life, Liberty and …the Happiness of Pursuit." As a base they used the famous picture of Marilyn with billowing skirts, to which the illustrator added a torch and a spiked tiara to make of her a Statue of Liberty!

Another example of this exploitation of existing still photos is a sweet one of Marilyn used as is but nestled in among a choir of singing young men in sailor suits. Its caption is "One in Every Crowd." What does it mean? A third is that of an airbrushed Marilyn (of course using the basic photo) scantily dressed in a black sheath and holding a severed ear. Behind her is the brilliant, apocalyptic night sky of the famous Vincent van Gogh painting. It is interesting that Marilyn, herself a practitioner of camp, should in her turn have become the object of camp that others latched on to.

Then there were the writers and poets whom she met: Carl Sandburg ("too bad I'm forty-eight years too old"); the Sitwells, Edith and Osbert; Aldous Huxley; Isak Dinesen; Norman Rosten; Saul Bellow, who thought her a witty woman; and Truman Capote, who danced with her.

Norman Mailer never met her, but wrote about her. Elton John sang about her after her death:

and Norman Mailer, obsessed with her, wrote two books and a play.

She married two American heroes: one sports—Joe DiMaggio; one literary—Arthur Miller.

She was presented to four heads of state: Elizabeth of Great Britain, to whom she curtsied; Nikita Khrushchev of the USSR, who crushed her hand so hard in greeting that her fingers hurt; Jack Kennedy of the United States, to whom she sang "Happy Birthday"; and Sukarno of Indonesia, who kept his eyes glued to her décolletage.

More ink, paper, film and developer were lavished on her than on anyone else of her generation, and more books have been written about her (there is a man in Florida who claims he owns 604 different ones); there have been stories, television shows, documentaries, an opera, a ballet, unnumbered magazine and newspaper articles, and films about her. Lucille Ball played a Marilyn skit with a blonde wig in an *I Love Lucy* episode. (Perhaps her only rival in the popularity sweepstakes is Elvis.) Marilyn acted in twenty-eight films.

She has come into the psychoanalytic literature.

Even if we allow for the flacks' apocrypha, it still is an impressive list of achievements during her lifetime and a measure of her hold upon the public imagination after her death.

he was named Norma after the silent screen actress Norma Talmadge and Jean after Jean Harlow. Her mother was a film cutter (her father she never knew). She was raised by a series of foster parents and spent two years in an orphanage which looked out over the RKO lot. From its windows could be seen the hillside on which is spelled out HOLLYWOOD in great letters.

All her life she was troubled by memories of emotional deprivation and poverty. She was a fabulist and liked to embellish, to make a story better, so it is hard to tell fact from fiction. There are tales of rape and maltreatment, but, whether real or not, they were real to her and she never escaped them. One story from that period was of the birthday cake wheeled out to celebrate the birthday of each child at the orphanage. It was a large cake covered in icing and bearing lighted candles. When "Happy Birthday" had been sung and the birthday child had made a wish and blown out the candles, the cake would be wheeled back into the closet whence it came. It was made of wood. True or false?

She was a special child, a gifted child who was thwarted, and she stuttered. Her escape became the movies. She would sit in the front row alone, watching the film unfurl three or four times until someone came to fetch her. Years later, in talking of those days, she would say ruefully, "And there was no popcorn either."

She was not able to judge the merits of the films. Whether good or terrible, to her they were instant magic. Her hero figures were Joan Crawford, Bette Davis, Jean Harlow, Gloria Swanson, Marlene Dietrich and Clark Gable.

She would return to the foster home or the orphan asylum and dream of herself on the silver screen. Her fantasies became her life. Enthralled by the Hollywood legend, she dreamed a world that became her fortress into which she would retreat and upon which she could draw when engulfed by the reality of her daily life.

She told me in 1960 when we were working on *The Misfits* that in her make-believe world Clark Gable was her father and that in her dreams he brought coloring books to the orphanage, not only for her but for her to give to all the other little girls. This tale she told while sitting with a set of proof sheets and a red grease pencil in front of her, editing pictures of herself playing a love scene with Clark Gable. She looked pensive for a moment, sighed and came up with another of her "can you imagine" sentences: "Can you imagine what being kissed by him meant to me?" She continued to talk of her childhood.

There must have been millions of movie-mad kids—bereft, shoved around, where do you go? You go to the movies, you fish movie magazines out of the trash. She was hooked. It took a prodigious act of will, and she had nothing but will, to become a movie star.

The movie magazines became her bible and her guide. Years later when she would be interviewed, she would be fearful of being misquoted. Roger Taylor in his book *Marilyn on Marilyn* has her saying: "I might never see that article and it might be okayed by somebody in the studio. This is wrong because when I was a little girl I read signed stories in fan magazines and I believed every word the stars said in them. Then I'd try to model my life after the lives of the stars I read about. If I'm going to have that kind of influence, I want to be sure it's because of something I've actually said or written."

Reared on the film magazines of the late 1930's and '40's, she would read publicists' extravaganzas about Garbo: "The Incomparable One," "The Flaming Icicle," "the supreme symbol of Inscrutable Tragedy" and "the mysterious, available but untouchable essence of the indefinable."

If Garbo was indefinable, the film scripts of that era were simplistic. Those plots must have influenced Marilyn: for instance, when she took Arthur Miller's father, Isadore Miller, as her escort when she went to sing "Happy Birthday" to President Kennedy. The movie star taking the old immigrant to meet the President of the United States. How's that for a Hollywood plot?

It was the movie magazines with their idealized still pictures that triggered her interest in photography. She would study the stars' images in *Movie Mirror*, *Photoplay* or *Screen Gems*, which were jammed with controlled glamour shots. She became familiar with every gesture, every plucked eyebrow, every dewy eye. So by the time she started posing for the still camera she was ready. She had imitated the stars in her mirror. Although her early stills are highly derivative, she was smart enough and skilled enough to find her own style.

There seems to have been an inevitability about her life as she started to prepare herself for the adult world. Although apparently she never deliberately set about creating the persona that emerged as Marilyn Monroe, a pattern reveals itself, a traceable progression.

She started with the shining smile, the almost Edwardian baroque figure, the breathless quality of voice (a device she used to cover the stutter), and she built on them. Because in her innocence she did not know things could not be done, she did them, and turned them—like the voice (her own was quite ordinary)—into assets. Her voice became a sexy purr, her walk became pure eroticism, and these, together with her open-mouthed lips, became bankable advantages. She learned to use makeup, experimented with hair styling, wardrobe.

Because she was poor, she wore blue jeans (an early popularizer of the now classic uniform) and a shirt. Her jeans she would put on moist so that they would cling more easily to her contours. Her dresses and sweaters, when she could afford them, she wore a size too small, to emphasize the curves, and she was an early wearer of the bikini.

In later years, whether she was in a ball gown, draped in furs or simply wrapped in her ubiquitous white terry-cloth robe, she had the knack of making the viewer think her completely nude beneath.

She was happiest in white, but would switch to beige or black for contrast. It was rare for her to wear color. In the early modeling photos she is still brown-haired, a pretty girl but not a knockout. When she becomes platinum blonde, everything else changes too. Suddenly there is a glow about her: skin, fingernails, toenails are all translucently silvery. Everything about her becomes exaggerated. Finding that her nose photographs a bit long, she learns to drop her lip so that the shadow cast by her nose seems shorter. This gives her a slight tremor, a look of expectancy that adds to the sexiness. Later she will add the pursed lips, the open mouth. This so affected her imitators that, going through fashion pictures of the '50's, you find yourself looking at so many open-mouthed models who seem to be gasping for breath that you wonder whether you've wandered into an aquarium.

Her imitators tried to re-create her walk too, but they never even came close to that swivel of the hips that was her hallmark. Like Chaplin, she built her film character around her walk. There is some question about how she developed it. In her starlet days she carried around with her a copy of Andreas Vesalius' book on human anatomy, so it was assumed that that was its source, because she insisted that she was studying the bone structure of the human body. She did learn a lot about the body—especially her own. (She kept herself in shape by lifting weights, running and walking.)

Ralph Roberts, her masseur, traces the walk to the time she was studying with Michael Chekhov. Either he or Lotte Goslar gave her a book called *The*

Thinking Body by Mabel Ellsworth Todd. Marilyn was a slow but thorough reader. She reported back to Chekhov that she hadn't understood one word. Chekhov told her to read it again, and again, and again. She did reread the book frequently and found in it an exercise to move from one buttock to the other while sitting. Roberts says the walk stems from this.

The walk called forth special words. Maurice Zolotow, who wrote probably the best of all the books about her—reasoned, intelligent, well researched— said "her lower back was marvellously callipygous." The dictionary meaning is having beautiful buttocks. Philippe Halsman talked of her "turbenoid undulations" and said that "rhythmically at the peak of its lilting tortillity it winked at me."

Billy Wilder was right when he said, "She does two things beautifully— she walks and she stands still." During a session, between takes, she often would walk normally. As with everything else about her (the smile, the voice, the glow), she could turn on the undulating hips at will. She would use them as a seduction tool or not—as she chose.

No wonder she often spoke of herself in the third person.

t was not just her physical self that she tried to develop. She began to buy books and records to try to educate herself. In 1952, when Philippe Halsman came to Hollywood to photograph her, he reported that she had at least two hundred books on her shelves ranging from James Joyce's *Ulysses* to Tom Paine's *Rights of Man*. There were e. e. cummings, Keats and Shelley, books on religion, history, psychology, translations of French, German and Russian classics. She kept Whitman's *Leaves of Grass* at her bedside and she enrolled at UCLA to take night classes in literature and art appreciation.

She confused learning with intelligence and was pained all her life by her lack of formal education. She was unlettered, but learned quickly from people she met. Her curiosity was a void to be filled, and she ingested information and experience. She had an instinctive understanding of people that enabled some of us to come close—but she always withheld part of herself.

Every book, every class, every new person from whom she could learn was a step up and out of the misery of her background. Her critics thought her reading a pose because during her starlet days she would walk about the commissary with a book under her arm. When she married Arthur Miller, a wise guy said she had married her college education.

She was ribbed unmercifully by the press when she told reporters that she wanted to play Grushenka in the projected film version of Dostoevski's *Brothers Karamazov*. She had read the book and understood the part. The later revision of opinion about her filmic skills indicates that she could have made a marvelous Grushenka. The movie was a dud.

She took lessons in speech, singing, dancing and acting, and she kept a picture of the great Eleonora Duse propped in a corner of her dresser mirror. Once when she was having a trying time on a film, I mentioned the fact that around 1916 Duse had made her only film and been quoted as saying that she had made the same mistake nearly everybody had made, that something entirely different was needed, and that it was a pity she was too old for the films.

Marilyn knew about Duse from her movie-magazine days. Garbo had been called the Duse of the Screen, and Marilyn knew about Duse's film. She explained that the mistake Duse alluded to was to treat the screen as though it

were a stage, where gestures have to be wide, facial expressions broad and pro-
jection intensified in order to reach the last rows in the upper galleries of the
theater, whereas in films exactly the opposite is required.

She worked at her craft, but spent thought and time trying to promote
herself. Often she was vague and seemed adrift, but she never lost sight of her
goal.

Finally she wangled a screen test. Leon Shamroy, the cinematographer
who tested her, was knocked out. His reaction: "I got a cold chill. This girl had
something I hadn't seen since silent pictures. She had a kind of fantastic beauty,
like Gloria Swanson, and she radiated sex like Jean Harlow. She didn't need a
soundtrack to tell her story."

The ability to project wordlessly in the visual vernacular made it possible
for her to be understood universally. On the basis of the test, 20th Century–Fox
took her on as a contract player. Then they started the usual starlet build-up.
They decided to call her the Woo-Woo Girl. She would appear as a starlet caddy
at a celebrity golf tournament or as a bat girl at a celebrity baseball game in
short, short white shorts and tight white jersey. Although celebrity games would
be played by studio actors to raise money for charity, they were intended as press
promotion for all participants.

She would go to parties to be seen, appear at luncheons for visiting
exhibitors, who took a shine to her and so helped to have the studio pay attention to her.

Often she would be overwhelmed with a sense of inferiority and shyness,
but would overcome it, turning her self-doubt into a style. "I would walk slowly
and turn my head slowly as if I were a queen."

The build-up continued: small parts were found for her; the studio photographers kept her posing for the flood of handouts to supply newspapers and
photo syndicates with black-and-white and color pictures.

Short items began appearing about her in movie columnists' space. A
short publicity biography was made of her: the theme was Cinderella in
Hollywood.

After all the hoopla, the studio did not pick up her option. Here her
appeal and her ingenuity came into play. A friend, Johnny Hyde, a powerful
agent, took her to John Huston, then the hottest director in Hollywood. She
read for a small part in *The Asphalt Jungle*; she wanted to read lying on a couch;
since there was none, she lay on the floor to deliver her lines. She got the part.

A photographer friend, Sam Shaw, took her to see Tom Prideaux, *Life* magazine's Entertainments Editor, who remembers that "she looked like a little street urchin, no stockings, no makeup; I'll bet a nickel she wore shoes, but it didn't seem so." Tom had seen her in *The Asphalt Jungle* and was intrigued with the contrast between the character she brought to the screen and the one who turned up in his office. She showed him her picture portfolio—sad little modeling shots, nebbish studio and location shots commissioned by the film-company publicists. Even this dross showed her shining forth and going beyond the material.

Months later the editor remembered her and had his movie correspondent in Los Angeles, Stanley Flink, take her to meet the Sitwells—Dame Edith and Sir Osbert—and Aldous Huxley. When Flink picked her up, she was stockingless. Prideaux says that, in honor of literature, she asked Flink to stop so she could buy hose to put on.

From the meetings with these editors came first a picture of her with seven other starlets; then, in April 1952, her first *Life* cover. The headline on the cover read "Marilyn Monroe, the Most Talked About in Hollywood."

This was her real launch. She was on her way to stardom, a position of precarious power, but through the rest of her life she would be the dynamo, she would generate the power, and she in turn would have to find the source of energy to drive the will to keep her at the top. For her this was always the public, through the use of the media, which she learned to manipulate with great skill. This gave her the sustenance she needed.

The beginning of my photographic involvement with Marilyn coincided with the start of the big time in her career. She was bouncy, full of plans and hope for her future. It was fascinating to watch her progress and see the cleverness with which she handled herself in those days.

The Asphalt Jungle was followed by *All About Eve,* where she held her own skillfully against consummate screen actors Bette Davis and George Sanders; in a small role she played a blonde actress without talent who is willing to do anything to become a movie star. Her convincing performance won her a seven-year contract with 20th Century–Fox. It was the only path open to her at the time, but it was to cause her anguish later.

In the ensuing years she battled the studio for her right to appear in films she felt suitable to her talent (she hated the dumb-blonde bubblehead she was expected to play). She fought for her right to choose her vehicles and directors.

She felt like an indentured slave. Although she had helped create the sex golem that took over her life (she really gloried in her sexiness), she resented being used as a sex object, a sex fetish.

With her later films—*Gentlemen Prefer Blondes*, *How to Marry a Millionaire*, *There's No Business Like Show Business* and *The Seven Year Itch*—she was producing millions for the studio, but was by Hollywood standards grossly underpaid. Her fight was not on the money level; her campaign was to force the studio to treat her like a woman and an actress, to give her a chance to pick her pictures and directors, and her strategy was to use the enormous impact she had at the box office as a bargaining tool.

Philippe Halsman said of her, "I saw the amazing phenomenon of Hollywood being outsmarted by a girl whom it itself characterized as a dumb blonde."

She herself said of Hollywood, "This is supposed to be an art form, not just a manufacturing establishment," and she used her dumbness with great shrewdness and turned her self-parody into a shining resource.

The studios are run on huge budgets, filmmaking is expensive, every minute costs, hysteria prevails. And into this world came Marilyn, difficult to handle, trailing her current drama coach and demanding retakes. I often wondered how much of her rebellion was getting her own back for the humiliation —real or imagined—she felt she was exposed to. She was clever enough to know that with her enormous following she was important to the film industry in its battle with television.

She left Hollywood and joined the photographer Milton Greene in New York to form her own production company, and she won her battle for choice of scripts and directors. The films she made in the ensuing years are perhaps her most memorable: *Bus Stop*, *The Prince and the Showgirl* and *Some Like It Hot*.

To obtain her ends, she flaunted her love affair with the public, more with men than with women. She used both planned public appearances and impromptu private appearances to create attention. She had told Maurice Zolotow in an interview that the public was the only family, the only Prince Charming, the only home she had ever known.

She wooed and won the multitudes. When she was lionized, she came alive; when she was told she was wonderful, she sparkled; and when she signed autographs, she glowed. She loved being the darling of the intellectuals, the icon enshrined in the workman's toolbox, and she loved to hear the truck drivers whistle. Her private delight was to get into a taxicab in New York and have the taxi driver swivel around, look puzzled and say something like "You know, ma'am, if you lost some weight, put on a little makeup and combed your hair, you would look exactly like Marilyn Monroe."

I watched her cause pandemonium in Bement, Illinois (see pages 50–51), and havoc in Brookhaven on Long Island (see pages 39–40). Just to lift a camera anywhere near her would bring out a mob. Being caught up in one was terrifying and downright dangerous, but for her it was proof of her existence.

It was the men who appreciated her most. She would play to them and they would respond to her blondeness, her sexiness, her warmth, her laughter, her provocation. En route to an appearance she would seem distracted, unaware of everything about her. Suddenly she would reach down into herself, call upon some inner resource, and it was as though by taking thought she had added cubits to her stature (actually she was quite small). Women would feel (without quite knowing why) either a kinship or compassion, hostility or anger (toward her blatant sexuality). People reacted either positively or negatively—but they reacted. Seldom were they apathetic.

There were the faceless numbers and there were the individuals who came forth to claim her. James Haspiel was one of the latter. He talked about her and the fans she attracted (including himself, in the third person): "There was the Monroe Six, her fan club, a half dozen kids who thought themselves exclusive—Jim was not considered by the others good enough—so he became a one man groupie." At sixteen, alone, he would wait for her outside her analyst's door five days a week when she was in New York—Monday, Wednesday and Friday mornings and Tuesday and Thursday afternoons.

Rejected by the six, the group Marilyn put together from two girls and four youths who would keep a vigil around her door rain or shine and would show up whenever she appeared in New York, Jim gathered his own folklore about Marilyn. One astonishing story: "The real Marilyn is yet to be discovered. She lived across the street from Eleanor Roosevelt. In those days Marilyn went to Larry Mathews, a hairdresser nearby who catered to show people. One day Eleanor Roosevelt was at the next dryer. They struck up a friendship and from then on they planned to come on the same day to sit next to each other and talk."

Jim Haspiel's flat in New York is now a repository of Monroe memorabilia in staggering profusion: early and late photographs, handwritten letters, photostats of birth and wedding documents, dresses, records, tapes, books, films. He himself has an encyclopedic knowledge of dates and events connected with her from birth to death—and after.

Sitting in the midst of his collection, he said in sepulchral tones of veneration: "Marilyn was working for me, she was creating her image, that's why I have to do a book giving her something. Norma Jean did her Marilyn for me."

In the end her audience believed that she did her Marilyn for them. She had the facility to seem to come close, to make contact, to have each person feel that she was putting on her show for him or her individually—it was an almost tactile quality.

Every encounter to her was a performance. This was particularly true with press and photographers. Always anxious for her image to come across as fresh and original, she would exhaust herself—she never held back, she never learned to save herself. The demands on her were great and she poured forth her gifts. This was to boomerang and become destructive, turning anxiety into fear, fear of ever-escalating demands on her strength—physical and psychic.

Also there was the normal fear of the free-lance: the feeling at the end of each film that there might never be another—and if there were, where was the strength to come from to sustain the talent? During the last years of her life, when she tried to pull back, it was already too late. The clamor she had set up would not be stilled. Right before her death, dismissed by her studio for unprofessional conduct—lateness and non-appearance while shooting her new film, *Something's Got to Give*—she went one last time to her public. There was one last burst of press interviews and photographs. This had been her most potent weapon and she knew no way to stop using it.

have tried to give headlines of Marilyn's life as I knew them to set the scene for the times when I photographed her. Since I knew her best from behind the camera and since the still photograph played an inordinately important role in her career and her life, it seems fitting to examine her through the lens.

Marilyn's greatest boost to stardom came during the era of the picture magazines, achieved with the aid of photographers. Words helped to publicize her, but photographs fixed the image firmly and indelibly.

Billy Wilder, who directed her in two films, said of her, "God gave her everything. The first day a photographer took a picture of her she was a genius." Whether this was said in irony or as a tribute, the truth is that she was not only a natural to the camera but that she had a sure knowledge of how to use that affinity. It was to her what water is to a fish—it was her element and she exulted in it.

As her celebrity grew, she was able to impose her authority, and she became her own director, her own star and, finally, her own editor with the power to reject or "kill" any photograph she disliked. This was not true of single newspaper photographs but of magazine editorial material. If an editor wanted her, he had to agree to her terms. She knew how she wanted to be seen, and if her cooperation was sought, she reserved the right of veto.

She knew she was superlative at creating still pictures and she loved doing it. She didn't have to learn lines as she did for her movies, she could let her imagination range freely without concern about consistency or continuity, she could be a different Marilyn for each photographer or each frame of film. It was always her party and often there would be champagne and music, but always total attention. It was she who in essence was saying, "Let's make a Marilyn." She may have invented Marilyn, but she had collaborators—lots of them: the still photographers. Yet she could call the shots, dictate the pace, be in total control.

Most personalities are uncomfortable with the penetrating eye of the little black box. It seems to reveal more than the filmic image, which is transitory and has sound to help it. The photograph is mute, fixed and stands on its own. It can be, as the Reverend Smith has said about photography, "justice without mercy."

I have seen seasoned actors freeze at the appearance of a camera. They say: "I don't have a line, I don't have a mark—let's block this out, tell me where to stand and what to do."

Not so Marilyn. She knew what to do. She would impose her psychic needs, her moods, her eroticism upon the session, working rapidly so that expression after fleeting expression wafted across her face, her body moving sinuously in cadence so that the photographer could only try to keep up.

She had learned the trick of moving infinitesimally to stay in range, so that the photographer need not refocus but could easily follow movements that were endlessly changing. Often she would seem a shimmering, molten wraith. She could be elusive, tantalizing. For each photographer she would be different, responding to the vibrations, but using herself and bringing forth different facets of herself.

At first I thought it was surface technique, but it went beyond technique. It was what John Huston called "truth." It didn't always work, and sometimes she would tire and it was as though her radar had failed; but when it did work, it was magic. With her it was never a formula; it was her will, her improvisation. She captured the imagination and heightened the atmoshpere.

Occasionally she would relax, but, no matter how much the photographer and the camera might try to recede into the background, she always knew where the camera was and what would be the most telling angle for her—and would unconsciously, almost imperceptibly, move into position.

The idea of the candid shot, the actress unaware, was impossible with her. She always knew—as though, wherever she was, whether in a dressing room, resting on a plane or walking in the desert, her own built-in mechanism sensed the camera and responded before the first click was heard. She didn't look in camera direction, she just knew and projected for a close-up even if there was a long lens trained on her that to others would have been invisible. It was like an unseen beam of light that only she picked up.

One photographer working with a long lens on a film set said she always knew where he was, even though he was stationed unobtrusively fifty yards from her. She would play to his camera, and then, when tired of the game, she would drop her eyes, her signal that she was through.

If it is true, as someone has said of her, that all her life she pursued a search for a missing person—herself—then perhaps Marilyn, a creature of myth and illusion, found herself not in the fleeting film image, but in the photograph, which would seem to give her concrete proof of her being. She could hold it in her hand, hang it on the wall, show it off. It gave her back herself. She was making love to herself, and we, the photographers, were there to record it.

In making the point of the contrast between her relationship to film and her relationship to photographs, Laurence Olivier, who starred with her and directed her in *The Prince and the Showgirl,* said, "Although she had undoubted talent, I think she had a subconscious resistance to the exercise of being an actress. But she was intrigued by its mystique and happy as a child when being photographed; she managed all the business of stardom with clever, uncanny, apparent ease."

As a subject she was unique, but there were days to make a photographer despair. She would look heavy, fat—as though if one put an apple in her mouth she could be served on a Christmas platter. Yet she photographed ten pounds lighter than she was—whereas most people photograph ten pounds heavier.

Another anomaly—her flesh. It was pneumatic, almost touchable on screen; she had what cinematographers call "flesh impact." Her skin was translucent, white, luminous. Up close, around the periphery of her face there was a dusting of faint down. This light fuzz trapped light and caused an aureole to form, giving her a faint glow on film, a double plus.

The photographer Burt Glinn said of her, "She had no bone structure—the face was a Polish flat plate. Not photogenic in the accepted sense, the features were not memorable or special; what she had was the ability to project."

She was totally uninhibited when posing, and all angles seemed to work. If she had a bad side, it was never evident because she would maneuver herself to avoid showing it; if accidentally it was exposed on film, it didn't matter—she would reject the finished picture. There was a sculptural quality about her. She was equally photogenic fore and aft, approaching or retreating. She could think of more ways to get herself psyched up for a picture shoot or an interview than anyone else I ever met. One way was to get out of the taxi two or three city blocks away from her destination, then run (usually with her publicist puffing behind her). She would arrive breathless, wind-blown, and manage to give the impression that she had just emerged from a delicious encounter with a lover.

Her makeup was a total mystery. According to "Whitey" Snyder, her veteran makeup man, she knew more secrets about shadowing her eyes and using special lipstick to make her mouth glossy than anyone else in the business. These "secrets" were kept secret even from him. But the routine of getting ready took so long that it would cut into the shooting time. The photographer might become irritable or impatient, but when Marilyn arrived, she brought with her the infectious ambience necessary to beguile, and away we'd go.

Posing was a game that she played with abandon and delight, drawing the other player, the photographer, into it with a silent but ever increasing psychic pressure. No word would be spoken, but she had made the connection, a tenuous thread that the photographer grasped, an umbilical cord that was sensitive, silent and tough.

Sometimes an almost trancelike atmosphere existed; then she would increase the tempo, the pace, until she was spent and it was suddenly over, leaving behind a mood of accomplishment. In an almost mystical way, we would have wrested from that roll of film a living experience that we had shared. It would feel like coming from watching a great stage performance—out of the darkened theater into the light. There was always a sense of bemusement when it was over.

It might have been easier to set a specific situation, to tell her what to do, to move her through it quickly, click-click and finish. This would have been efficient, but would have had pre-ordained results—no surprises. It would have missed the unexpected spark and stifled the chance of freshness that only she could provide.

I do not work that way. I work intuitively, trying not to impose myself. I let the person come through. I am the medium. She too worked intuitively. We were both gamblers, risk-takers, and we took chances. We both trusted ourselves and each other to carry us through.

In Milton Greene's *Women and Their Elegance*, Norman Mailer invents for Marilyn one of his "factoids": "I who always feel I know the inside of a camera the way other people are familiar with the inside of their stomachs."

I don't know what other people know about the inside of their stomachs, but I do know that Marilyn knew nothing about the camera beyond the fact that it was bliss. The technology was not for her––she worked on instinct, and her instinct served her well. She didn't need to know the technicalities. She knew that she could create what fed the camera, and that was her special ability. It was the unpredictable in herself that she used. What she had to offer cannot be taught—there are no rules, and if there were, she would have broken them.

ware that over a stretch of more than thirty years one's memory is far from unclouded, and that one's perceptions change, I have gone back to source material of the period for both words and pictures. I found my own notes, impressions of each shoot, as well as text, captions, contact sheets, prints and transparencies. I unearthed contemporary interviews, writings and photographs of photographers in front of whose lenses she had appeared: Cartier-Bresson, Philippe Halsman, Cecil Beaton, Milton Greene, Bert Stern, Richard Avedon, Doug Kirkland, Bruce Davidson and John Bryson. I interviewed Inge Morath, Burt Glinn and Ernst Haas.

I looked at thousands of photographs, not only by these professionals, but by many others. Since amateurs too had a field day with her, I looked at and checked their pictures where possible. I developed eyestrain from the number of stills I saw: publicity, studio, documentary, production, news, editorial, personal—color and black-and-white.

When I sat down to absorb all I had seen and read, it became plain that at every stage of her adult life, from the age of eighteen when she had had her first professional photo session (with David Conover of the Armed Services for *Yank* magazine—his commanding officer was Ronald Reagan) on the assembly line of the parachute factory where she worked, there had always been photographers. To Conover, taking these pictures may have been just another day, but for Marilyn Monroe it was a turning point.

She quit her job and started to model. Posing for her first magazine cover (*Family Circle*, Spring 1946), she is dark-haired, wears a pinafore and cuddles a baby lamb. On her next assignment she poses with a crippled child for the March of Dimes. When we move on to her first studio portrait, she is blonde, demure, smiling, and one nude shoulder peeps out. We next see a new genre for her, the "girlie mags"—*Swank, Peek, Click, Laff, See*. In these she is coy, not salacious even when scantily clothed or in a swim suit.

Modeling jobs came in fast succession. She worked at industrial shows, did a commercial for Union Oil, was in demand for photographers who could always use a pretty girl to pose for them and went off to Washington State with André de Dienes to do a picture series.

Next step: the movies. She was signed by 20th Century–Fox for one year. She spent most of her time on publicity stills—at the beach, in the park, in the mountains, in the gallery, on the backlot. It was the time of the Korean War and the studio kept her busy filing requests from the troops for "cheesecake" pictures. Along with the avalanche of stills the studio was releasing, it also started a campaign to get newspapers and magazines to send their own photographers, and it contacted independent photographers to invite their participation.

There followed a fallow time for Marilyn when her contract was not renewed. Then she did *The Asphalt Jungle* for Metro-Goldwyn-Mayer and she was in demand again. Philippe Halsman came to Hollywood to photograph eight starlets for *Life* and Marilyn was one of them. His notes say: "I photographed each in four basic situations—listening to the funniest but inaudible joke, enjoying the most delicious but invisible drink, being frightened by the most horrible but invisible monster and finally being kissed by the most fabulous invisible lover."

Marilyn failed in all but the fourth, but in that one, Halsman goes on to say, she gave "a performance of such realism and dramatic intensity that not only she, but I was utterly exhausted."

The following year *Life* sent Philippe back to do a cover story on her. This *Life* cover was to change her life. She was no longer a starlet. The power of the press had made her an upcoming movie star. She had possibilities of becoming a major star. Her salary was adjusted, she got a better car and better living quarters.

Halsman, probably rightly, took credit for being the first to photograph her walk: "Some of my friends say that in trying to capture Marilyn's personality I discovered—for the American public—her derriere."

The night before Halsman's *Life* cover session with Marilyn, he and Stanley Flink, *Life*'s West Coast movie correspondent, called on Harold Lloyd to see a remarkable collection of three-dimensional photographs he had made. When they told him that next day they would be photographing Miss Monroe, he asked for permission to join them with his stereopticon equipment.

Next day they all assembled in Marilyn's tiny one-room apartment. Stanley Flink described what took place. Halsman and his assistant set up the light and put the Hasselblad on a tripod on a special platform. Lloyd perched on a camp chair with his gear. Flink, a tall man, tried to stay out of the way, and Marilyn posed wedged between a dresser cabinet and the bathroom.

The door was kept open to try to cool the room, which had gotten pretty hot from the photo lamps.

Marilyn, a bit tense, kept scratching her fingernails against the woodwork. Halsman, who liked to keep provocative chatter going through the take, threw questions at Marilyn: "When was the first time you had anything to do with a man? How old were you?"

Marilyn continued to scratch. "Six," she said.

"How old was the man?"

Marilyn kept worrying the woodwork: "Younger."

Lloyd, roaring with laughter, somersaulted backward through the open door into the hall.

They got their cover.

By the time the *Life* feature was ready for publication, the story about her nude calendar pictures had broken. Nowadays if Nancy Reagan did it, it wouldn't raise an eyebrow, but those were puritanical times and it caused a scandal. *Life* cannily added the nudes to their story, thus in a way legitimizing them.

Marilyn had posed for the nude calendar (called "Miss Golden Dreams") in 1949 and was surprised when it came back to haunt her and cause difficulties. These were the days of the Hays Office censorship, and briefly it looked as though the studio would ban her, but wisely they decided to acknowledge the truth about the nudes and cash in on the publicity.

She had earned $50, the photographer $900, and the company that bought and distributed the pictures earned millions. They were referred to as "the shots seen around the world" and by 1963 eight million calendars had been sold. They were copied onto everything from posters to coasters.

The pictures were exploited in three ways: The nude, sold *au naturel*, was intended to go into workmen's toolboxes, into men's clothes closets, into sports locker rooms or wherever a man might comfortably hang a nude. The second-stage nude had a brassiere drawn over her breasts with red hearts over the nipples. This was intended for more elevated viewing: in men's clubs and bars. The third-stage nude was for home consumption and general release. Over the nude was painted a black chemise which covered her to mid-thigh.

The next photographer to affect the course of Marilyn's life and her career was Milton Greene. He came to Hollywood to photograph her for *Look*, but stayed to convince her to become her own producer. As her partner, with forty-nine percent of her company, he helped her in her strife with her studio.

Together they wrested from 20th Century–Fox her right to choose (from a list of twenty) her directors and her right to have a say about what films she was to make.

They were young and ambitious and each believed the other could work miracles. She adored the pictures he took of her. To me she said that he knew more about color, lighting and photography than anyone in Hollywood, and that with him she would have a chance to develop as an actress and make the films she wanted to make. He believed that producing a film was not too different from running a photo studio, and that together they couldn't fail.

He found the money to support her during the year and a half she was in New York on suspension while they were negotiating with 20th Century–Fox. When she went back to work to make *Bus Stop* with Josh Logan directing, Greene was hired to design the lighting and her makeup. He was responsible for the way she looked in the film—a pale, honky-tonk "chantootsie" who looked as though she lived under a rock. He did a brilliant job. She looked just right for the part of the blonde, very touching floozie.

By the time they went to London to make *The Prince and the Showgirl*, on which he was executive producer, their relationship was beginning to deteriorate. She was beginning to feel that parting with forty-nine percent of herself was too much, and he felt that handling her solo had been easier than handling her after her marriage to Arthur Miller. The making of the film was fraught with difficulty, and when they returned to America they knew it was time to part.

At the time of the announcement of the making of *The Prince and the Showgirl*, Cecil Beaton photographed Marilyn for *Harper's Bazaar*. It was a picture that she cherished. It is slightly grainy, as though it were a color shot that had been transposed to black-and-white. In it she looks about sixteen years old and she holds a rose in her hand. Of her he wrote: "Miss Marilyn Monroe calls to mind the bouquet of a fireworks display, eliciting from her awed spectators an open-mouthed chorus of wondrous 'Ohs' and 'Ahs.' She is as spectacular as the silvery shower of a Vesuvius fountain; she had rocketed from obscurity to become our post-war sex symbol—the pin-up girl of an age. And whatever press agentry or manufactured illusion may have lit the fuse, it is her own weird genius that has sustained her flight."

But it was perhaps Richard Avedon, of all the photographers who surrounded her, who made the series of pictures that pleased her most. They were done on assignment for *Life*, but they were reproduced worldwide. She re-created the great sex symbols of other eras: Jean Harlow, Clara Bow, Lillian Russell, Theda Bara and Marlene Dietrich. Done in color in the style of the period, they are glamorous and, as with Marilyn's counterparts who were photographed in earlier days when film was slow and they had to freeze, they are static. She loved those pictures and admired her performance for Avedon's cameras. She kept repeating that she wished her movies were as good.

Simone Signoret wrote in her autobiography:

She irritated me too, Marilyn. It was a bit tedious to listen to her tell about how happy and inspired she had been during the months when she made that series of photographs with Richard Avedon. The series was, indeed, remarkable; they were pictures of her made up to impersonate all the big stars of the thirties. But listening to her, you'd believe the only satisfaction as an actress she had ever felt was during those disguises, when she suddenly turned into Marlene, Garbo and Harlow. She talked about these photography sessions the way other actors talk about their films. She seemed to have no other happy professional memories. None of those moments of uproarious giggles among pals, none of those practical jokes, none of the noisy hugs and kisses after a scene when everyone knows all have acted well together. All these things were unkown to her. I couldn't get over it.

What is interesting about her on stills is that, no matter how the photographer tried to use her in terms of his own personality and style, it is always she who imposes herself to have the final look. Even in Avedon's pictures, with their heavy overlay of props, clothes and backgrounds, she is not stifled. She comes forth as the projected character—Marlene or whoever—but the picture is also unmistakably Marilyn herself.

During the time of Marilyn's suspension in New York, I was photographing Joan Crawford and her daughter Christina for a women's magazine. I had never met Miss Crawford and was excited at the prospect of photographing her. Our first meeting was set for an afternoon of clothes buying and fitting at the showroom of Tina Leser, a famous dress designer.

Joan swept in, kissed me on both cheeks, deposited with a secretary two live tiny pissing poodles she sported on her wrists and burst forth: "I have just come from the Actors Studio, where I saw Marilyn Monroe. She had no girdle on, her ass was hanging out. She is a disgrace to the industry."

I knew that Joan Crawford, the movie idol of Marilyn's childhood dreams, had hurt her deeply recently when she attacked her in the press for conduct unbecoming an actress, after Marilyn had appeared and been photographed (actually the photographers had buzzed around her like bees around a honey pot) at a gala in a brilliantly colored dress that was so tight that Marilyn had had to be sewn into it. Crawford went on to talk to me about herself. *She* was a lady; she laughed and said that one owed one's public consideration and that when she went out even to buy sanitary pads she wore white gloves. But Marilyn was a disgrace, and the nude calendar—wasn't that an offense against respectable women everywhere?

When we went into the dressing room, Crawford said she was ready and she started to strip. I hurriedly said that perhaps we had better wait for her daughter Christina, since my editors wanted a two shot. But I was too late. There before me was Crawford naked. Too inexperienced to know how to handle the situation, I photographed her—in the nude.

Years later I pieced it all together. Crawford had started her professional life making pornographic films, had spent the first ten years of her stardom buying them back (some still surface). That day she had been heavily into the 140-proof vodka which was her constant companion. I still haven't figured out how much of her "nudie" act was pure reflex and how much was fury and competitiveness with Marilyn's nude calendar shots.

I interject this anecdote as an illustration of just how Marilyn's being always in the limelight, being always able to garner the attention of photographers (even when she posed in ways that her detractors disapproved of), brought her even further attention.

Marilyn tried not to let the malice or anger of occasional detractors spoil her enjoyment of the huge popularity that was hers. She continued to enjoy the picture-taking periods and applying what she learned from these sittings to her film work. Laurence Olivier, who had his difficulties with her on *The Prince and the Showgirl* and who hated being photographed (I know—one of the most wretched afternoons of my life was spent doing a cover of him for *Newsweek*), said of her in his autobiography: "She would always do exactly what was asked of her by any stills photographer. I marveled at first at this show of discipline and thought it augured well; my reaction only a few weeks later would have been: 'Well, of course—she's a model.' I think that wherever she gleaned that particular training, it taught her more about acting than did Lee Strasberg."

John Springer, who worked with her in New York and was responsible for some of her personal publicity, remembers: "You could talk to her about her most recent film which might have been a triumph and that was all right, she was happy about it, but talk to her about her most recent magazine picture story and she positively glowed with pleasure."

It was not just the photographers that turned her on, it was the amateurs who were her public that delighted her heart. She would pose for almost anybody who had a box Brownie with the same grace and skill she gave to professionals.

When the pros and the amateurs turned out en masse at the filming of *The Seven Year Itch*, there was bedlam. The scene was Lexington Avenue, New York, in midsummer and hot; she stands over a subway grating to cool off, and as the subway train rushes by, it lifts her white dress and swirls her skirt above her thighs. The actual time was midnight, when Billy Wilder, the director, figured the streets would be empty and he could deploy his crew and get the shot done. But the publicists had leaked the word, and depending on your source, there were six hundred—no, six thousand—amateurs hanging out of windows, clutching high up at telephone poles, stuck on rooftops. Wherever one looked there was a camera, and of course there were the professionals with their tripods and their paraphernalia in a spot assigned them. Here, too, the statistics vary, from fifty to five hundred. There was also the film crew, the police, assorted relatives and gawkers.

It was impossible to work. Every time the train thundered by underground and the skirt blew up, the amateurs surged in from behind their barricades to elbow out the pros. Equipment was disturbed, tripods were knocked over, tempers flared. The popping flashbulbs of the amateurs made it impossible for Wilder to work. Finally he made a pact with the amateurs: If they would stand back and permit the professionals to work, he would set up a few shots for the amateurs so they could get theirs.

This was a happy occasion with a happy solution. There were other occasions that were less serendipitous. Marilyn's divorce from DiMaggio and her marriage to Arthur Miller brought out the paparazzi aspect of the press. At times in her life when her privacy should have been respected, there was no way to stem the flood of words and pictures that had become part of her daily living. She was to grow to hate the beast that took upon itself the right to be privy to everything that happened to her.

During the time of the DiMaggio divorce, not only did the regular press congregate in her yard for three days, trampling down her lawn, but at the divorce court a miserably sad Marilyn was greeted by a mob of people interspersed among the press, shoving and pushing and throwing questions at her about the break-up of her marriage.

Before her wedding to Arthur Miller the interest in her was of a vicarious intensity hard to believe. The domestic press was augmented by the foreign press, and whenever the couple got into a car, motors revved and the chase would be on (shades of every motion-picture pursuit: "Driver, follow that car"). Near Mr. Miller's home in Roxbury, Connecticut, the New York bureau chief of *Paris-Match*, Mara Sherbatoff, was killed. Her car had plowed into a tree while following Marilyn and Arthur. Before the ambulance arrived and while she lay dying (and Ira Slade, her driver, sat weeping and praying), the photographers, temporarily diverted from Marilyn, stood over her, clicking away.

Even then the madness didn't stop. Marilyn went to England to make *The Prince and the Showgirl* and to have her honeymoon with Arthur Miller. Here, outside the manor house bordering on Windsor Great Park, the property of Queen Elizabeth, photographers hid in the trees, their telephoto lenses trained on the master bedroom to try to "grab" a picture of the honeymooners.

It is hard to understand Monroe mania. Why should her pictures disappear from files? Why did prints Josh Logan made of her disappear from his house, to be followed by the negatives going missing? Who cuts out her pictures from library books? Who stole my transparencies of Marilyn nudes? Probably all taken by respectable people who ordinarily wouldn't dream of despoiling a volume or of stealing my pictures of Mamie Eisenhower or Margaret Thatcher.

What did she mean to her own time?

Over dinner in New York recently, irritated by finding that some of the library material I sought about her had been vandalized, I asked my brother, Jack Cohen, that question. He is exactly the age Marilyn would have been, an able economist knowledgeable about marketing and trends. He called her the Hula-hoop of her day. A good answer, but the Hula-hoop disappeared and she lives on.

It is easy to say that commercial interests are stimulating sales of artifacts about her, but it isn't enough to say that people are buying because others are selling. People are buying because she fulfills something in them, because they want to buy. Is it the same impulse that triggered her and her generation to look at movie magazines? The search for heroes, for icons?

What made ordinary people feel as though they had been anointed when they were momentarily admitted into the inner circle to be photographed with her? Three examples: When she was married to Arthur Miller, she miscarried and had to be rushed from Amagansett, Long Island, to Lenox Hill Hospital in New York. Her doctor traveled with her, and when the ambulance arrived, they were greeted by a swarm of reporters and photographers. The doctor was photographed with his patient when she was being wheeled into the reception area. This enraged the doctor. Next day he called the publicist and told him off; he thought the picture-taking an obscenity and a slur on his profession. After the doctor hung up, calls kept coming in to congratulate him. How did it feel to be photographed with Marilyn Monroe? Wasn't he the hero, though? The doctor, bolstered by his publicity, called the publicist back. Would the publicist arrange a press conference for the doctor? Perhaps more pictures with the star.

The second story concerns one of the members of the House Un-American Activities Committee who were responsible for interrogating Arthur Miller, asking him to name names before being willing to issue him a passport. Miller stood firm. No names. Then the committee member offered a deal: If he, the member, could be photographed with Marilyn, no more questions would be asked. Again the playwright stood firm. No pictures.

The third story was told by Joe Wohlhandler, Marilyn's personal publicist during the Miller years. When she appeared on stage in Chicago at the premiere of her own production of *The Prince and the Showgirl*, she overwhelmed the press and the city. It was a triumph and everybody wanted to meet her. Mr. Wohlhandler introduced his brother-in-law, an academic at a university. "She posed for a picture with him and he became big man on campus. He has lived on it since 1957. For all I know, he may have received his tenure because of her."

Why does she continue, as Sammy Davis, Jr., puts it, to "hang like a bat in men's minds"? And it is the generic "men," because after her death women, too, adopted her. What is it that speaks to the young of the present era, people unborn when she was alive? It may be true that fame is timeless, but that can't be the answer. Perhaps we should just accept the phenomenon and enjoy it.

If the "why" is not traceable, the "how" is. The how is television, the medium that she helped battle when it was in its infancy. It is ironic that the "box" is largely responsible for her ongoing popularity. There is a further irony in that she seems to come off better there. The small-screen image has the feeling of a still photograph, a closeness and touchability that she strove to achieve with her audience. It seems a more intimate way for people to be able to tap into her fantasies.

lthough the *Esquire* story had been her idea, it took Marilyn a long time to get around to it. I was involved with more serious projects—McCarthyism, the Black Muslims, poverty in the American South—so although I was intrigued with the idea of photographing her, I turned the logistics of the sitting over to the people at the magazine to arrange, and she seemed to recede into the background.

Then one evening during late summer, while walking on the beach near my home at Miller Place, Long Island, I saw Norman Rosten approaching with a blonde girl. We said hello and I waited to be introduced. In the dusk with the light behind her, it was hard to recognize the glamorous Marilyn I had met at the party in New York. Without the high heels, the makeup, the nimbus of public personality, it could have been any pretty, plump, blonde girl. Her hair was a mess, blown by the salt spray. She looked small and remote. She apologized for the procrastination in getting the *Esquire* story going. She said, rather appealingly, that she was anxious to do it, and wound up by suggesting that we all meet for a swim the next afternoon. There seemed a tacit understanding that this was to be a social gathering.

When we came to the beach at the appointed time, her hosts were there but she wasn't. I had thought about bringing my cameras, and then thought that she probably wanted to be incognito and that the cameras would embarrass her, so decided to leave the pictures for a more professional occasion.

I felt a stir all along the crowded beach. People were turning to look at Marilyn moving slowly down a cliffside from the meadow above our heads. She was wearing a bikini of sorts—tight, short, white balloon-cloth bottoms and a bifurcated brassiere, each section barely covering a breast and supported by a narrow band at the base. There were string shoulder straps to hold it up. On her head she had a huge natural-colored straw hat, and for footgear she had found a pair of men's army boots—government issue.

It was a hot Saturday afternoon in August and the whole town and their weekend guests jammed the beaches. There were three sections, two private ones separated by a public area. The small private beach that we occupied was, according to the town code of riparian rights, supposed to be inviolate, but this in no way stopped our neighbors from either walking along the waterline or swimming along it to investigate the apparition in our midst.

Within seconds of Marilyn's touchdown on a white towel on the pebbly beach, the place exploded with activity. Adults swam from the public beach and lined up at the water's edge to gawk at her. Children ran over, clutching bits of charcoal and stones they had found on the beach ("My mother said please write your name on this rock"). Behind the phalanx of gaping people drawn up as though for close-order drill, speedboats came in to shore to see what the excitement was all about. And in a circle to one side stood the men in our party, up to their knees in water, talking and smoking. Later it turned out that they were conjecturing as to whether her breasts had silicone implants.

After a few moments of embarrassment, the amateur photographers whipped out their cameras and started snapping away at her. In the middle of this hubbub the photographer from the weekly newspaper, the Port Jefferson *Times*, arrived. I was seething because I hadn't brought a camera. I wouldn't have shot because it would only have added to the confusion, but it was a terrific situation and a frustrating one.

The local photographer came up to me and, seeing me without my gear, thought the whole thing a gag. "Somebody said that's Marilyn Monroe. That ain't Marilyn, is it?" he asked.

"Why don't you ask her?"

Perplexed, too shy to ask and muttering, "That ain't Marilyn Monroe," he went off down the beach, swinging his Speed Graphic.

At this point Marilyn got up to play softball with my five-year-old son, Francis, and his friends. When she had had enough of this activity, she decided to go into the water. By now the men had finished their discussion and joined her. As she started to swim, her crowd of admirers followed suit and surrounded her. For a moment it looked as though they would drown her, they were so tightly packed around her.

Someone raced to a telephone at the nearest house and called the harbor police. They arrived smartly in a speedboat and rescued her, smiling and waving to the crowd. She had set the town on its ear and loved it.

The foregoing is taken from my notes written the afternoon of the beach scene. But, in *Rashomon* fashion, there are conflicting memories. To check to see whether there was anything I missed, I talked to other people in the party who had shared that afternoon, and I reread Norman Rosten's account of it in his book on Marilyn.

We more or less agreed on everything but the rescue. Rosten remembers that the afternoon gave him a chance to play hero. When everybody surrounded Marilyn in Long Island Sound, he "struck out blindly, furiously, and seizing her by the arm started swimming out into deep water." He kept her afloat until somebody came along in a boat and took her away.

Lou Achitoff remembers that when she went into the water, primarily to try to get away from the mob surrounding us on the beach, the mob followed her and the situation became nasty. It was at this point that a private boat came alongside her (he says it could not possibly have been the harbor police, it would have taken them over an hour to get there) and she got in. There were only she and the man, and an hour later she came limping back to the Achitoffs' house on the cliff, where we all had foregathered.

Sandy Achitoff remembers the rescue the way Lou does and she also remembers other bits and pieces of trivia from that weekend which have stayed in her memory bank for thirty-five years. One was that while the rest of the party ate and drank their way through endless meals, snacks, and drinks, Marilyn dieted on cottage cheese and at one sitting consumed a pint carton of the stuff; another was that when everybody went "skinny dipping" by moonlight, Marilyn was the only one who kept her bathing suit on; and the third was that the town still remembers the Marilyn weekend as "the biggest thing since Helen Twelvetrees."

For weeks afterward the local drugstore was developing amateur films of Marilyn Monroe while I still hadn't got my first picture.

erhaps the irony of the local "snapshooters" having a go while the professional stood by appealed to some perversity in Marilyn's sense of humor, or she may have begun to trust me that mad weekend, appreciating the fact that I understood her well enough to stand by and not complicate her performance— because it was a performance. Also she knew that *Esquire* was eager for the picture essay it had assigned, and maybe she did want to see how she would look in *Esquire* compared to Marlene Dietrich, as she had told me.

Whatever her reasons, when the magazine called the following week, she said she would be visiting the Rostens over Labor Day and would be happy to set up a session then. My problem was to find a place to work where we would avoid the furor of her last visit. She would arrive on a holiday weekend, the last one of the summer, and the beaches would be impossible unless we worked at dawn or at dusk.

It would be a mistake to try to impose a time schedule on her. Also the location would have to be close by so that we took no chances of being on the public roads where she might be recognized. An abandoned children's playground and a deserted marshland in the neighboring town of Mount Sinai would have to do.

It was not possible to pin her down to an hour at which to start work. Each time I phoned, she said, "Tomorrow." Finally, on Monday, the last day, she agreed to work after lunch and then kept dawdling over some cottage cheese, a conversation with Hedda Rosten, makeup, doing her hair and, of course—woman's eternal question—what to wear. The answer was bathing costumes. All of this was fine because if she prolonged it just long enough, we would be on time for what filmmakers call the "magic hour" when the whole world seems golden.

By the time we got to the playground, it was pushing five. She worked quickly and efficiently, looking appealingly, vulnerably, at the camera. It was an experience to watch her seduce the camera. (Years later Dame Margaret Rutherford, the marvelous British comedienne, said while watching her at work on a soundstage in Hollywood making *The Misfits*, "She makes love to the camera." The grip who was standing by said, "You're right, ma'am, she fucks the camera.")

She would do it all; the photographer had only to watch out for the proper angle, the play of light and the technical necessities. She directed herself.

Sometimes I would tell her what was wanted, but usually only give an indication; she was in control, setting the style and pace, and I would follow, just praying that my reflexes would be fast enough to accommodate to her antics. She had an enormous sense of play, a delicious sense of fun which was at once irreverent and elusive. It was amusing to watch and to follow where she led.

The timing for the marshes was just right, the light soft and shadowless and ranging from pale yellow through deep saffron.

In the car Marilyn had changed into an imitation-leopardskin bathing suit. The idea of the leopard in the bulrushes appealed to her sense of comedy, but neither one of us was prepared for the fact that the landscape which had looked so lovely from the road was marshy. The farther we moved into it, the more swampy it became. But this did not deter Marilyn. She was intrepid. She stood in it, sat in it, lay in it until the light started to go and I called a halt. She climbed out, covered in mud, but she was exhilarated—and she was giggling.

My main problem had been to keep my Nikon cameras from getting muddy. As usual, I had three—one draped around my neck, and one over each shoulder. The one around my neck had a "normal" lens—a 50 mm; another a 35 mm (the closest to a wide angle I will allow myself when I photograph people, feeling that the photographer has a responsibility not to distort the person who lends her face); and of course there was my portrait lens—a 1:05 mm.

The reason for the three cameras is to be able to work quickly and easily without having to pause to change lenses or cameras once contact is established between the person in front of the camera and the person behind it.

or these first pictures of Marilyn, I used color—then still a novelty in editorial photography. It seemed right for the time of day, her blondeness and what we were both trying to express. Dietrich I had shot in black-and-white, and to Marilyn her being in color represented a kind of one-upmanship. Color was being used more and more for covers, but a color picture story was still new enough to please her. She said that although she always thought of herself as blonde all over—just blonde monochrome—her blondeness was more exciting in color.

In the early '50's, color was still in its experimental stage and little was known about the properties of the film itself. It was slow, with a rating of first 8 ASA, then 12 ASA (consider the fact that it is now possible to go to a speed of 2,000 ASA). Even less was known about color reproduction, but editors were anxious to be ahead of their competitors in the field, and photographers were anxious to find out more about the new technology. I was an early color pioneer, beginning with covers and then going on to picture stories.

Among my colleagues, a controversy arose about the merits of black-and-white versus color. The purists would say that color is commerce and black-and-white is art—an argument that has not abated with the years. And there were those who would snidely say that if color had been discovered before black-and-white, there probably wouldn't have been any black-and-white at all—and then what tack would the "artistes" have taken?

As for me, I am greedy and, not wanting to limit myself, will use whatever tool is at hand. So, depending upon the dictates of the mood and the moment, I will switch from color to black-and-white and back again, or will manage both simultaneously—a trick that becomes increasingly difficult to handle. It is interesting that at the beginning of our working together I shot Marilyn in color; in the intervening years the various sessions were in black-and-white; and toward the end, even though *The Misfits* was filmed in black-and-white, I shot both.

Perhaps here it would be appropriate to talk about the picture magazines of this period.

The 1950's in America found a lively, competitive magazine market for pictures: *Life, Look, Collier's, Saturday Evening Post* were the big general maga-

47

zines; *Esquire*, the sole men's class magazine; *Vogue, Harper's Bazaar, Ladies' Home Journal*, the important women's magazines; *Time* and *Newsweek*, the news magazines. There were also magazine supplements as adjuncts to newspapers, a raft of second-string and pocket-size magazines, as well as specialty magazines like *Holiday*.

In those days people got their visual information from periodicals. Historically, we photographers were the forerunners of television—the innovators of many of the formats later adopted by and adapted to that medium.

There was an amusing postscript to the Long Island take. Marilyn had asked to see the pictures, and, being too inexperienced to know that most photographers do not show their results to the subject before publication unless it is specifically agreed beforehand, I went to the Waldorf, where she was living, to show them. She had said on the phone that she had a woman from a European magazine coming to interview her at four, and if I didn't mind coming a few minutes earlier and sitting through the interview, she would look at the pictures afterward.

When she opened the door of her suite, she was wearing a diaphanous, totally see-through black negligee, her feet were bare and she was holding a hairbrush in her hand. In a few minutes the interviewer arrived, and when she was seated and looking into her bag for notebook and pencil, Marilyn asked the woman if she minded if she brushed her hair.

"Of course not," the woman replied, and when she looked up, Marilyn was brushing her pubic hair. The woman was so startled that she sputtered her way through the interview and left very quickly.

When the pictures were projected, Marilyn was enthusiastic about them. There were one or two that she felt not quite right, and I agreed to destroy them.

The Mount Sinai pictures of Marilyn were published in 1953 in America and were distributed fairly widely abroad. It had been an amusing thing to do, but I saw no particular reason to repeat the exercise. Occasionally we would run into each other in New York at parties and we would chat. Once she came into an ice-cream parlor run by Michael Field, the cookbook writer. It was the fashionable thing to do at the moment, and they knew each other.

As Marilyn made her entrance, a vision in white, she was approached from the opposite end of the shop by her arch-imitator, Jayne Mansfield. As they passed, each stared fascinated at the other, then seemed to slither past—and one could imagine two sinuous snakes taking stock of each other. There were no darting tongues, but one imagined them.

There were a few magazine requests for me to photograph her, but either I was busy or she was not available.

Sometime in the spring of 1955 she called me at four o'clock one morning to tell me that at ten that morning she would be flying out to Bement, Illinois, a town where Lincoln and Douglas had debated, to "bring art to the masses." Would I join her? There would be only she and her hairdresser, Leonardi, and I could have exclusive pictures. Curious and half asleep, I agreed.

At the airport she cavorted about the outside of the plane for the benefit of the photographers. In the crook of her arm was a large hardback book of Carl Sandburg's about Abraham Lincoln. She was with Carlton Smith, head of the National Arts Foundation. He had convinced her that the people of the small town of Bement were having an art exhibit and that she would be the one to introduce art into their lives. Actually, the town was celebrating its centenary and Marilyn was to be the focus of nationwide publicity just by showing up. It was really a con.

All the male inhabitants over the age of puberty had grown beards for the occasion and were to appear in a tableau. On the plane Marilyn was asked to write a speech about Lincoln to deliver in Bement. Lincoln was a hero to her. She had met Carl Sandburg and he was a hero to her, too. Years later she was to say that it was Arthur Miller's resemblance to Lincoln that first attracted her.

By the time we reached Chicago she had written her speech and was rehearsing it; as she whispered the words of the talk about "our late, beloved

President," it sounded as though Eisenhower, not Lincoln, had just died.

It took all day to get to Bement. First stop Chicago, two-hour wait there, change planes for Champaign, then an automobile cavalcade with the governor's own motorcycle escort to Bement. It was a nightmare: the press, radio and even embryonic television had been alerted. Total chaos. Everybody wanted to see her, to talk to her, to get her autograph, to touch her. By this time she knew she was being used, but she was game, joked with the press, posed for pictures, signed autographs and smiled for everybody.

Wherever we went, the press of people was so great that in order to give her privacy I stood guard at the ladies' room in the airport. I had long since decided that I would try to document the craziness of her junket and the kind of mass hysteria she engendered. Also, if I could catch the mood of her behind the scenes, that would add immeasurably to the story. Many times we were caught in the crowd and it was not only impossible to use a camera but it became impossible to breathe. The crush was really frightening.

She rode it all with aplomb, but when she got to Bement she was frazzled. She had a kidney ailment for which she was later to have an operation—something doctors describe as a disease of women fair, fat, flatulent and forty. She was precocious, she was in her twenty-ninth year. To keep the illness at bay, she had to take a daily dose of tablets. In her excitement she had left the pills in New York, so now her ankles had swelled. She asked for a basin of water to try to get the swelling down and she lay down on a bed with her feet raised above her head. She rested, ate grapes, while her hairdresser, resting his head against the bed, fell asleep. Meanwhile the old house where we were in Bement was surrounded by people. They were peering into windows (some of which had no blinds), knocking on the walls and calling out to her.

She had not brought anything to change into, so I ironed her dress while she did her makeup, had her hair done and brushed up on her speech. Then she put on a pair of short black gloves and went forth valiantly to "bring art to the masses."

She met the hirsute men, looked at the art (a few pieces of primitive art on loan from a Chicago museum—into one a sheaf of wheat had been stuck to give it that middle western look), spoke her speech, had another endless series of radio and newspaper interviews for local media and prepared to leave.

Here she hit a snag. The plane that was to have carried us back to New York couldn't take off. There was a storm brewing and the small plane couldn't fly above the weather. What to do? Carlton Smith said we would have to spend the night. She looked so crushed that I stepped in. Surely planes were flying out of Chicago, and we were only eighty miles away. Couldn't one of the cars that brought us from Champaign drive us to Chicago? Problems. No. Smith couldn't commandeer the governor's car (he was anxious for her to spend the night); we would have to call Springfield and get the governor's permission. First call Chicago. Yes, there was a plane at eleven that night for New York. Yes, they would hold seats. We had exactly one and a half hours to make it to the airport. One of the motorcycle men got the governor's office on his walkie-talkie, we were granted permission and away we went, official car and motorcycle outriders racing toward Chicago.

The evening had turned cold, and Marilyn was freezing in her thin, sleeveless dress. She looked frozen, so forlorn, so like a sad child that I took off my sweater and put it around her. The plane was on the tarmac, waiting for us. The governor's men had held it for ten minutes. Then the hairdresser, Marilyn and I staggered onto the darkened plane. It was a flight that had originated in California and most of the passengers were asleep. Nobody recognized her. Her hair was tangled, she was just a tired, ordinary girl.

It had been a taxing day for us all. We had enplaned at La Guardia Airport at ten a.m. and we arrived back there at two the following morning, but we had had to rise early to get there. Marilyn had come from Connecticut, I from the north shore of Long Island. She was on display all day and had to keep touching up makeup and having her hair adjusted to make sure that she looked good for the various local papers—but even more important was the story for my camera, which was for a European magazine release.

She would watch the person photographing her—even if it was just a small-town newsman. She had learned that frequently the national press picks up from local wire services and she would perform at her best for all. With me she started to let down just to get a break, but if she sensed that I wanted more from her, she gave it in good measure.

If I felt she was flagging and it was necessary, I would say what was wanted and she would swing into action. Mainly what was wanted was for her just to be herself. This was hard for her to do when there was a camera in evidence. She was so conditioned by years of "cheesecake" that at the prospect of an audience or a camera she would react almost automatically. The breasts would come forward, the bottom would swivel, the smile would start lighting up the eyes and

Marilyn was "on." She was at her best in the motorcade from Champaign to Bement, waving and laughing—Hollywood royalty on the move. Unfortunately, it was not possible for me to photograph it. I had to go along in the one car provided for our party. When we arrived at our destination, I tried to get back far enough to take pictures, but was almost knocked over by the crowd pressing in. I was admonished by the police, who made a path for me, but so great was the curiosity about her that those people who had not been able to raise their cameras in the crush to get to Marilyn contented themselves by photographing me and asking for my autograph! Just being associated with her gave me special status.

When we parted in New York, she hugged me and thanked me for intervening so that she didn't have to spend the night in Illinois—clearly, she was touched by my solicitude. I felt we were beginning to be friends.

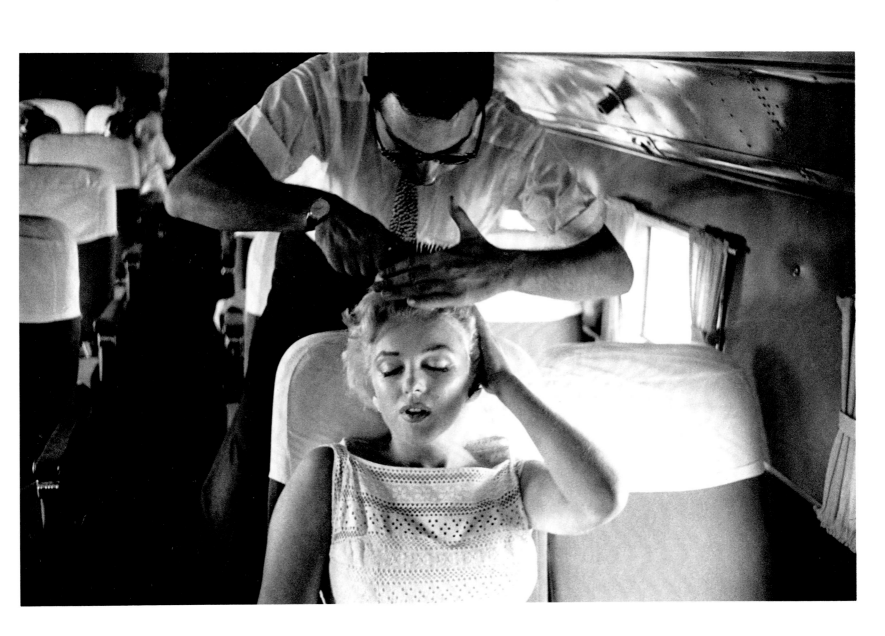

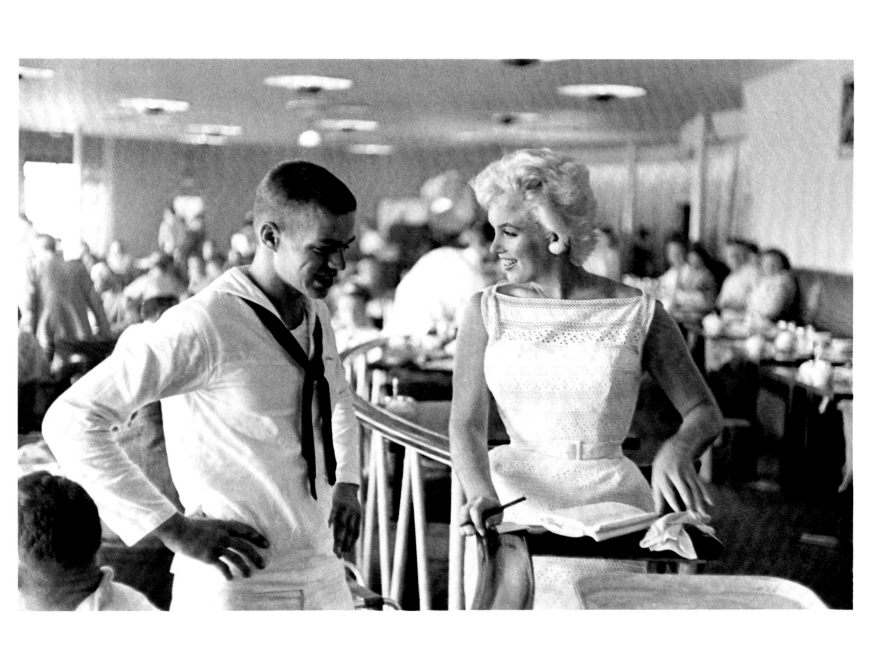

BEMENT, ILLINOIS. MARILYN EXAMINES (TOP) A PRIMITIVE
STATUE, POSES (BOTTOM) WITH A BUST OF ABRAHAM
LINCOLN FOR AN INTERVIEW AND MEETS (FACING PAGE)
THE LOCAL INHABITANTS.

AT THE END OF THE
LONG DAY IN BEMENT.

n 1956 Marilyn was much in the news. She had married Arthur Miller, she had formed a company with Milton Greene to produce her own films and she had contracted to make *The Prince and the Showgirl* with Laurence Olivier. There was an overwhelming amount of publicity about her. The unlikely combination of the intellectual playwright and the sexpot movie star who was, for the most part, identified in people's minds with the role of dumb blonde that she played in many of her films captured the imagination of the world press.

It was a year since the trip to Bement, Illinois, when her East Coast publicist, Lois Smith, called with an invitation to attend a press conference at the Waldorf for Sir Laurence Olivier, as he then was, and Miss Monroe to talk about their new film to be made in England. Please to come a bit early to see Marilyn in her dressing room before it all started.

Marilyn had always had difficulty before actually tackling a problem. Once she started something, she would be totally committed: it was the business of propelling herself into the actual situation that she had to grapple with. She was aware that she would have to generate the energy, create the magic and excite the imagination of her reviewers. It wasn't as though she were merely on exhibition, speaking someone else's lines. She usually made up her own lines, spoke her own ripostes, created her own persona, and she always feared that her personal act might reach a point of diminishing returns. So she would vacillate, the minutes passing, people waiting and getting angry. Time became her enemy, but she seemed paralyzed, unable to do anything about it in spite of the fact that she didn't want to alienate anyone.

Here she was, about to go on show again—so different from the bedraggled waif who had boarded the Chicago plane a year ago. At eleven in the morning she wore a black velvet gown with straps the width of spaghetti strips. She looked lovely, her white flesh and blonde hair contrasting with the darkness of her clothes. When I complimented her on the way she looked, she winked at me in the mirror and said, "Just watch me."

I stayed only a minute to greet her. She was already late, and outside in the anteroom were Sir Laurence and the author of *The Prince and the Showgirl*,

Terence Rattigan, sitting together uncomfortably on a small settee. They glared as I hurried toward the elevator and the upcoming press conference.

First Marilyn appeared with Olivier, Rattigan and Milton Greene. They were on a balcony and below them was the press. Slowly Marilyn and Olivier came down the stairs and were engulfed by the crowd of professionals who were friendly, but because of the swarm of people it was difficult to get through. They finally sat down at a table and the questions started. At first Sir Laurence gravely and seriously answered. Then Marilyn settled in, removed her coat, leaned forward—and broke one of the thinner-than-thin straps. Suddenly the atmosphere changed—she had made it fun: laughter was heard, a safety pin was offered and the press conference was hers. It had gone from a ponderous, humdrum, expected situation to an event—with a little help from her.

The hundreds of press people, word and picture, who had turned out to see Marilyn with the famous British actor were delighted with her. They felt that she had handled the "accident" of the broken strap with style. Remembering the wink in the mirror and her "Watch me," I was amused by her cleverness and glad that I had come.

Normally I would have given photographing a press conference a miss. It was the kind of routine public event I try to avoid, but after last year's junket to Illinois I was "hooked" on Marilyn. She piqued my sense of humor, and although I hadn't much hope for anything special in the way of pictures, I went to see how she would handle herself.

Photographically her press conference was so jammed as to make it almost impossible to work. Between exploding flashbulbs and pushing photographers intent on the one necessary "shot" to fill an afternoon news slot, the feature photographer is always at a disadvantage. The feature photographer needs something special that will tell more than the obligatory record shot does. For this, space to move and a chance to wait for the right moment (which may never come) are essential.

Ordinarily there is only one angle from which the newsmen work, so that they are usually bunched up directly facing the subject. The newsmen (there were very few women photographers in the '50's) were always unfailingly courteous to me. Invariably a path would be made for me. My five-foot-two-inch height was no threat to them. They could shoot over my head and they knew that I wouldn't abuse their help by shoving. So there I was, way out front to get my pictures and to watch Marilyn do her stuff.

or months before principal photography started on the John Huston film *The Misfits*, publicists were busy beating the drums about it. Arthur Miller had written a valentine for his wife, Marilyn Monroe; Clark Gable was to co-star with her; Montgomery Clift, Eli Wallach and Thelma Ritter were to be in the supporting cast. The producer was Frank Taylor, a book publisher and editor. The word was that with these disparate talents and with Marilyn having had her choice of both director and co-star, something special could be expected.

The motion picture was to be shot in sequence—an expensive way to do it, but one that gives the actor a better chance to concentrate on and to build his film character as the movie unfolds. It was to be small-screen and in black-and-white (the last expensive film to be made that way—the category no longer exists in the awards lists) to emphasize the intimacy and humanity of the plot.

It was to prove to be an extremely difficult film to make. Briefly, the story is about three roistering, wandering, hard-living, macho characters who make their living in cowboy country, riding in rodeos and rounding up wild mustangs to be sold for dogfood. Enter the girl—Marilyn—who is to change their lives. On screen Clark Gable becomes her lover, Montgomery Clift her "soul mate" and Eli Wallach her friend. The script deals with their growing relationships as the men go about their daily business of heavy drinking, rodeo, flying about in their decrepit airplane to find wild horses, and winds up with Marilyn's horror when she realizes that the wild mustangs will have to be killed to be turned into dogfood.

Magnum Photos arranged for the exclusive rights to all still photographs on the film. This meant that only our agency would be permitted to take pictures not only during filming but for any picture stories the actors might agree to do away from the location. We alone would supply the world's newspapers and magazines with material.

It was agreed that the photographers would go out in pairs to Reno, Nevada, the base from which the film was being made, and that there would be a change of photographers every two weeks, thus giving a degree of continuity while guaranteeing variety. At the time this seemed to make sense. Instead of every magazine sending its own people (and they would have totaled hundreds before the film was finished), there would be only two biweekly picture takers and our own caption writer, Dick Rowan, who would be there for the duration of the filming. He would also be responsible for getting the proof sheets of pictures approved (the principal actors had written into their contracts the right to "kill" photographs they didn't like).

There was enormous interest in Clark Gable starring with Marilyn. When added to this were Miller's script and John Huston's direction, the requests for editorial coverage from both the United States and abroad were overwhelming. The arrangement with Magnum was calculated to take the burden of having to relate daily to different photographers from the shoulders of the actors. It was done particularly to free Marilyn of all extraneous concern.

The film started in a spirit of goodwill and happy expectation. Eli Wallach said it was like having the Fourth of July every day. It was "and they lived happily ever after—for two weeks." Into their early honeymoon came the first two Magnum photographers, Henri Cartier-Bresson and Inge Morath.

According to Inge, it was fascinating to watch the difference with which Marilyn related to the two of them—male and female. Both of them were captivated by her. She flirted with and played up to Henri; with Inge she was just very sweet. Each of them viewed her differently. To Inge she was "a photogenic phenomenon. The thing about her was you could not photograph her badly if you tried. Once she was ready [to be photographed], she would surpass the expectations of the lens. She had a shimmering quality like an emanation of water, and she moved lyrically."

Inge photographed her rehearsing her dance in the moonlight. "It was poetic—not classical. Normally when she saw a still camera, there was an automatic reaction—the bosom lifted, the bottom stuck out—but with the dance it was all poetry and grace. She was master of the still camera—she was the animal trainer and the photographer was the beast. She always struggled with the film camera, but with the still camera she was free."

If she was a photogenic phenomenon to Inge, to Henri she was an American phenomenon. Henri Cartier-Bresson is a legend in the history of photojournalism, a narrative poet in photography, if you will, an innovator, a shy, reclusive man whose greatest wish is always to remain anonymous so that he may not intrude upon the territory of his own pictures.

All his life he had shunned publicity, so it was all the more surprising that when he left Reno he did an unprecedented thing for him: he left behind a taped interview about Marilyn and his experience with *The Misfits*:

I saw her bodily—Marilyn—for the first time and I was struck as by an apparition in a fairy tale. Well, she's beautiful—anybody can notice this, and she represents a certain myth of what we call in France "la femme éternelle." On the other hand, there's something extremely alert and vivid in her, an intelligence. It's her personality, it's a glance, it's something very tenuous, very vivid, that disappears quickly, that appears again. You see, it's all these elements of her beauty and also her intelligence that makes the actress not only a model but a real woman expressing herself. Like many people, I heard many things that she had said, but last night I had the pleasure of having dinner next to her and I saw that these things came fluidly all the time…all these amusing remarks, precise, pungent, direct. It was flowing all the time. It was almost a quality of naïveté…and it was completely natural. In her you feel the woman, and also the great discipline as an actress. She's American and it's very clear that she is—she's very good that way; one has to be local to be universal.

By the time Inge and Henri left Nevada, the atmosphere of bonhomie had started to give way to tension, then to worry, and finally to deep concern about whether it would be possible to finish the picture, because, although there had been meticulous planning, everything seemed to be falling apart. In the end, the company survived and the film was completed, but a planned fifty days of production and a $3,500,000 budget came in at ninety days of production and $500,000 over budget.

The sheer physical environment was daunting: there were difficult scenes to shoot on a tough desert location at Pyramid Lake, a dry lake sixty miles from Reno, where cast and crew were housed. The daily trek of sixty miles each way meant getting up early and returning at dusk after the light was gone —six days a week.

When the film was begun in early summer, the afternoon temperatures would range between 100° and 110° Fahrenheit, and when it was finished in the late autumn, winter weather had begun to set in and braziers for warmth had to be set up in the desert. Then the winds would become strong in the afternoons and blow up sand as fine as pumice that would irritate the lungs, redden the eyes and produce dry coughs. The high winds bothered the horses and made filming them troublesome and sometimes dangerous.

If the location had its hazards of extremes of heat and cold, dust storms and wild mustangs, long hours, fatigue and boredom, the home base, Reno (Just the Biggest Little City in the World) had its own risks: gaming tables, "one-armed bandits," bar girls, prostitutes, all of which provided recreation as well as gossip, the life blood of every film crew.

But the big gossip was always, Would Marilyn work that day? She was worn out from her last film, unhappy that the Yves Montand affair was over, and that her marriage to Miller was ending. In the drama behind the drama, it was sad to note that Miller had written the short story that formed the basis for *The Misfits* in Nevada while waiting for his divorce from his first wife. Now he was in the same place and his marriage to Marilyn was over. It was hurtful in the early film scenes to see Marilyn on her way to the divorce courts. But in spite of the strain the Millers were under, she would often turn to him for help with the film, and he tried heroically to keep things going. But she could be cruel too. As her problems multiplied, she stepped up her intake of drugs, and she found it increasingly difficult to show up for work.

In the initial planning, the producers had built in as many safeguards as they could think of to make it easier for her to function. She had Paula Strasberg, her coach and friend, to help with lines and to give her a sense of confidence (the film company gave her an extra $3,000 a week which she in turn gave to Paula). In order to avoid the daily hairwashing, setting and drying, wigs were used for most scenes. The time schedule was adjusted for her benefit so that shooting did not start until noon most days. And still there would be days when she couldn't make it at all.

Of course during the difficult times the photographers shared the problems with the others. Frank Taylor tells of a set-up Elliott Erwitt contrived in order to induce Marilyn to pose for a group shot, a picture that she had kept putting off:

"I was endlessly concerned about getting a group shot (Huston, Taylor, Gable, Miller, Monty Clift, Eli Wallach and Marilyn Monroe), but every time I suggested it everyone threw up their hands in horror—the thought of trying to assemble everyone seemed impossible.

"I suggested it to Elliott Erwitt and he said he had an idea—so he rigged up a set-up with ladders, boxes, stools and parachute silk. It was on the location and he stretched out getting it ready for three days—he created enormous curiosity about it, but refused to tell anyone what it was about. He picked a day when everything seemed to be going smoothly—he asked us all to convene—it was probably a lunch break or when we were waiting for the sun to appear from behind a cloud—he just gathered us under the silk—Marilyn and Monty were intrigued and played around and joked—it was fun and spontaneous and suddenly it was done."

I was among the last of the Magnum people to go out. My two weeks were to stretch into two months, until the film was finished. It had been decided that it would be easier on Marilyn to have me, whom she knew and trusted, stay on so she wouldn't have to adjust to new people every fourteen days. She was in a very fragile state. She had taken an overdose of sleeping pills and been removed to a hospital in Los Angeles, where she had been under treatment for a week.

When the plane I was traveling on touched down in San Francisco, Marilyn got on with Arthur Miller and her secretary, Mae Reis. She had on one of her outlandishly large straw hats and, as usual, caused a stir. She was returning to the location in Nevada after her stay in the hospital.

The film company, anxious to hush up the overdose story, had a big Hollywood hoopla waiting for her when she disembarked, even though it was midnight. There was the local band and banners saying WELCOME MARILYN and applause from practically the entire company, who were there to greet her. I tried to slip away without being seen, but she saw me and made a point of saying that she was delighted we would be working together again.

Ernst Haas, my Magnum colleague, had already arrived, but he had arranged to do a special story on the wild horses. He was in the midst of his important study of motion and how to capture it in stills, and he was besotted by the mustangs. This gave us each our own territory and left me free to spend time alone with the actors.

Recently Ernst talked about the atmosphere that surrounded *The Misfits* when we were there: "All the people who were on the film were misfits—Marilyn, Monty, John Huston, all a little connected to catastrophe, Gable not saying much, just himself being Gable.

"It showed how some stars are like stars in heaven that are burned out. The light is still traveling, but the star is gone. They were actors playing out the allegory, then seeing it in life. It was like being at your own funeral."

Perhaps a bit drastic, but many days did have a sense of loss, of failure, of decay.

The conversation with Ernst reminded me of the problems I encountered as a photographer on *The Misfits*. It is customary for a film to have a production photographer whose function it is to record each scene. With the rise of the picture magazine, the "special" photographer was added—usually a fairly prestigious practitioner, brought in to bring a fresh eye and create interesting photographs and picture stories about the making of the film. This material, it is hoped, will be so compelling that magazines and newspapers will not be able to resist publishing it. More often than not, the "special" (which I was) is engaged by the film company but also assigned by one or more magazines, which expect their own exclusive stories. It helps if the photographer is also a journalist.

It is a tough spot to be in—to try to keep one's integrity and still give value for money. One walks the tightrope between the needs of the film's promoters and the needs of the magazines, one's own view of the subject and what the subject is willing—or able—to give to the camera. In a much less exalted way, it is reminiscent of the position of the artist under the great patrons of the Renaissance. Here in our democratic and commercial world we find our space between the advertisements. In a sense, the producers of goods for sale are our patrons.

I was relatively inexperienced, having only once worked on a film set—a *Life* picture essay on Joan Crawford—and had still to figure out relationships and adjustments, to distinguish what was possible from what was not possible, to understand how a movie got made.

The photographer is actually in the way during filming, and has to figure out a *modus vivendi* so as not to become a nuisance. The set always seems booby-trapped with hazards. One has to avoid standing in front of lights, tripping over cables, getting into camera range—especially when wide-angle lenses are being used—tripping the shutter (on the camera) when sound is running, casting shadows and especially getting into the actors' eyeline.

How the photographer overcomes the difficulties and manages to get pictures depends on the director. If he is welcoming or even tolerant of the photographer, then usually cast and crew will fall in line.

On *The Misfits*, John Huston was marvelous to me. Very often when he saw me hanging back in the shadows, not wanting to get in the way, he would bring me closer to camera position so I could photograph, and when we worked on the camera car for the scenes with the wild horses, he made sure that I had a good spot on it before he got up to direct.

Since what was required photographically was a sense of what went on behind the scenes off-camera, the best—and also the least disruptive—way of working was to "shoot" through the rehearsals and between "takes." This meant hanging about from the moment the cast and crew started makeup and lighting to the end of the day when Tom Shaw, Huston's first assistant director, called out in his gravelly voice, "It's a wrap."

The notion the public has that filmmaking is glamorous is totally erroneous. Except for the few glorious moments when a scene is filmed in which everything comes together, everybody's efforts pay off, and there is a sense of real community, the rest is grinding boredom. This sad truth was best expressed by Jimmy Stewart years later when we were working on a film called *The Flight of the Phoenix*. It was noon in the blinding heat of the Arizona desert and we were waiting for the "sparks" to light up the desert and for the sweepers to cover up their tracks. Stewart said he had been in films for thirty-five years and had acted in seventy movies, and he then started to calculate the number of hours it had taken various crews to get things ready before he could start working in the years he had been a star—and he said wryly, "I figure I've been waiting two and a half years." Those months on the Nevada desert, it seemed that each day we waited an eternity.

When Marilyn greeted me on location the morning after our arrival, she was very sweet, but wanted immediately to know how she looked. She looked radiant and I was happy to tell her so. It was four years since we had worked together and she looked at my face for a long moment to make sure she could still trust me. Then she drew in her breath, sighed and said, "I'm thirty-four years old. I've been dancing for six months [on *Let's Make Love*], I've had no rest, I'm exhausted. Where do I go from here?"

She was not asking me—she was asking herself. I felt her pain, but the only thing I could do to try to ease that pain was to photograph her—to try to recapture the pleasure she felt when we worked together. It was a game we had always enjoyed. I hung around photographing while she studied her lines, and she seemed at peace.

That first day she had a scene in the Dayton Bar where she was to dance with Montgomery Clift. At first she rehearsed the dance with Eli Wallach. Then Eli danced with Angela Allen, the script girl, then with Marilyn's stand-in, Evelyn Moriarity, so Marilyn could see the action. Then Arthur Miller stepped in to dance with Marilyn the way he said his father had danced. The jukebox blared out "Skip to My Lou, My Darling," and there was a sense of jollity in the room. It was hard to think of the question asked earlier in the day or to remember that Marilyn had taken too many sleeping tablets the week before.

That day there was a sense of relief and optimism on the location. A new Marilyn had returned. Perhaps things would work out after all—the picture would be finished.

The sense of reprieve didn't last long. A scene next day between Marilyn and Monty Clift called for pages of dialogue and lasted for five minutes, the longest Mr. Huston had ever directed. It was played in the yard behind the Dayton saloon against a mound of wrecked automobiles and empty beer cans that had been gathered by the local schoolchildren. It was to go on in blinding heat, rehearsal after rehearsal, take after take, for two days. Tarpaulins had been stretched overhead to try to keep out the heat and to diffuse the sunlight, and broken car seats had been provided for the actors to sit on. Still, when the 10,000-watt lights were switched on, the flies buzzing about, and the stench vile, it was like some nether hell. To expect anyone to concentrate under these circumstances was diabolical.

Marilyn and Monty had become close friends. She kept calling him "Brother." They were tender with each other and protective of each other. When the flies became so bad that repellent had to be used, she would put her hand over his eyes. He would make bad jokes to make her laugh. At one point she was concerned because his jeans, his costume in the film, sagged. She told his dresser to make sure that Monty put them on moist so they would be a tight and sexy fit.

Always with Marilyn there was the difficulty of learning lines. It came hard to her, especially since there was a great deal of rewriting overnight or during filming and she would have new words to learn at short notice. She struggled valiantly, but it must have been frustrating to her to see the three men, who were all seasoned actors, scan the new words, absorb them, then go before the camera word-perfect.

Her unpredictability was understandable but hard to take. Her moods shifted like clouds passing across the sun. Her friendship with Eli Wallach, which dated from her early Actors Studio days in New York, underwent a change. They had been close friends, but she would suddenly grow cold on him. One day she would sit on his lap or he on hers, and the next day she would cut him.

With Gable she always was at her best—considerate, gracious and amusing. One day when there was too much sun for a day-for-night shot and everybody sat around waiting for a cloud to cover the sun, Gable told her he was expecting his first child. He was almost sixty and thrilled about it. She was very happy for him and it was touching to see them together at this moment. I knew what they were discussing—Gable had confided in me earlier in the week when

Kay, his wife, had driven out to the location with a cradle in the back of her station wagon. He had asked me to say nothing until Louella Parsons announced the impending birth in her column. (Having lived all his Hollywood life cautiously treading between La Parsons and Hedda Hopper, the two powerful movie columnists, in order to offend neither, Gable had Parsons make the announcement about the child but chose Hedda Hopper as its godmother.)

Marilyn's relationship with John Huston was one of awe. Having him as her director again was a dream come true. He had been responsible for casting her in the first film in which she was noticed, *The Asphalt Jungle*. He was her talisman. He treated her in the same courteous but distant way he treated all his actors. When he directs, he is an Olympian figure. A writer himself, he is always deeply involved in the script; a painter, he plans the look of the overall film; an actor himself, he then leaves the interpretation to the actors in front of the camera. To some actors this is unsettling—they expect to be directed—but he feels they should pull it out of themselves. But if the actor needs help, he will give it.

Marilyn's uncertainty may have demanded more instruction than he gave, but he kept her thinking and working on her role. She tried to please him, and in the love scene on a bed with Gable, when he, fully dressed, woke her with a kiss, she, nude and covered only in a sheet, sat up and dropped the sheet. Showing her breasts nude was not in the script—it was her own notion of how the scene should play. When you consider that this was 1960 and frontal nudity was a rarity in films, she thought she was doing something praiseworthy.

Huston let her finish the scene her way, didn't say "Cut" to the cameraman until she was through, but he did cut it in the editing. And when she looked at him for approval, all he said was "I've seen 'em before." He didn't feel they belonged in the film he was making.

When the producer wanted to enlist her help in keeping the scene in the picture, she thought it was natural and said, "Let's get the people away from the television sets. I love to do things the censors wouldn't pass. After all, what are we all here for, just to stand around and let it pass us by? Gradually they'll let down the censorship—sadly, probably not in my lifetime." The shot was not used in the film.

It is interesting now, in thinking about Marilyn and her relationships with the people on *The Misfits*, to go through the contact (proof) sheets. There must be a dozen instances of her touching, hugging, sitting on laps. With the advantage of hindsight, it seems like a cry for help.

After the nightmare days of the beer-can scene—and before it had to be reshot—there was a bit of a respite, and, like evanescent images in a kaleidoscope, moments keep coming up on the screen of my mind.

One was a scene in which Gable, drunk out of his mind and bringing Marilyn and Monty behind him, erupts through a door of the Dayton saloon onto a street. He is looking for his children to introduce them to his friends. Weaving and yelling, he jumps up onto a car and falls off to the other side. Gable had insisted upon doing his own stunts and it was a very moving scene. The sixty locals who were hired as extras for background to the scene, and Kay Gable, who seldom came to the location, all applauded when he was through, but the look of wistful tenderness on Marilyn's face was something special to remember.

Another day that stays in the mind was one in which Marilyn was to plant some flowers at the Stix house (where the four characters were living). Gable kept calling them heliotropes, the only name for a flower the character knew. It was a lovely cool September day. The sun shone through blue skies. Everybody was in good humor. Marilyn was early for her 10:30 call. But by afternoon we were waiting again. Everybody lay about on the lawn in attitudes of abandonment.

Next day she was in a playful mood. She, Monty and her masseur, Ralph Roberts, were fooling around—making a pyramid, massaging one another. Throughout the film the one memory that remains constant is of people massaging each other's shoulders as though all the tensions and problems of making the film had settled there. She wasn't often easy and jokey with people the way Gable would be, playing childish pranks like attaching a horse-tail to Angela Allen's back or just relaxing with a joke, so it was good to see Marilyn in this kind of mood.

While we were still at the Stix house location she came to a lunchtime birthday party for Russ Metty, the cameraman. She had been changing, but appeared in her terry-cloth bathrobe and insisted we do a group picture with all of the crew who were there at the time. Knowing that Mr. Metty was important to the way she looked on film, she had established a special relationship with him.

Our next location was Pyramid Lake, in which she was to go for a swim wearing a skin-colored bikini bathing suit. It was a scene she had been looking forward to and she talked about it teasingly, but nobody seemed interested. It was sad to me to see her put on her sexy act for the crew, who by now were so fed up with her lateness and the disruptions to the film that their professional pride was offended and they just didn't respond. Whether she was aware of this or not she never said, and of course I never asked.

During the filming I divided my photographic time between Gable and Monroe. Gable, once he accepted me, was very easy—the ease that comes with professional security and success. Marilyn, by contrast, although she accepted me and regarded me as a sort of picture Boswell who was welcome even in intimate situations, managed often to project her anxieties so that I couldn't help being caught up in her mesh of tension and distress. The monotony, the waiting and the emotional drain of the diplomacy required to keep Marilyn amused and sufficiently interested so that she would want to sit for pictures away from the film location created more of a strain than the physical demands of the job, although they were taxing, too.

As always where close contact was essential to the personal kind of pictures I wanted to make, I worked without an assistant. Lugging gear, loading film, reading exposures were tasks I could have been relieved of, but an extra person might have unbalanced the precarious equilibrium between us. It was a matter of being endlessly on the *qui vive*, of being aware of Marilyn's problems and difficulties, of being sensitive to her wants and needs, of being able to walk away at the wrong moment, of sensing when to press at the right moment.

Being a woman helped me understand her moods and responses. Also, my being another woman avoided the male-female byplay that my male colleagues tell me is necessary in their sessions to produce intimate pictures. The myth has always been that it is necessary to go to bed with the subject. I have no way of testing this claim, but, knowing a little about the state of Marilyn's psyche during the filming of *The Misfits*, I would guess that such a relationship would only have added to the problems.

As the film moved to its end, the most difficult scenes were still ahead and the weather, as it progressed toward winter, made the matching of the film increasingly difficult to achieve—after all, they had begun photography in mid-July and it was now October. Jim Goode, who wrote a meticulous chronicle called *The Story of The Misfits*, records Frank Taylor's reaction to this stage of the proceedings: "Everything was happening at once: animals, truth, climax and revelation, but everyone's energy is going downhill when it should be going up."

This was indeed the climax of the picture, the episodes with the wild horses.

Before we got into these heavy scenes, I asked Marilyn if I could set up a party for her and any guests she might choose to ask. The purpose was threefold—to say thank you to Marilyn for her cooperation, to try to lift her mood before she went into her difficult scenes, and to create a situation for some pictures away from the daily filming.

I waited until a Friday night when she had had a productive day of work, then suggested the next night, Saturday, knowing that Sunday was a free day and we would all have a chance for a lie-in. She was enthusiastic and said she would like to bring her entourage and Montgomery Clift, but made a point of saying that no one else was to be asked—a sharp way of making me understand that Mr. Miller was not to be included. I hastened to reassure her that it was to be her guest list and her party, and she was to issue invitations herself.

She was pleased especially when I told her I had made arrangements at the Country Inn, which was in a private house in Virginia City. We would have the whole place to ourselves. She had dined there before and liked Edith Palmer, the woman who ran it. I told her that I would take care of the menu and all other details.

Next morning at ten Paula Strasberg stopped me to say that she would be unable to attend because she expected a headache at six that evening. It seemed perverse and ungracious and I teased Paula about it, but she was adamant that the headache would arrive. It was only recently that I learned that at the time she was mortally ill with the disease from which she eventually died, and that her headaches did worsen at day's end.

She was a strange figure in black, loose-robed taffeta, a costume completed with a conical-shaped hat like the dunce cap of old. She kept saying that she wanted to be invisible, but her get-up was a very strong silhouette against the stark desert sandscape. Occasionally if things were going well, one of the crew would sneak up, having first rubbed a hand in the sand, and place the hand on her rump, leaving the fingered outline for all to see. Behind her back they called her Black Bart.

She was in an unenviable position with the crew and the other members of the cast. They weren't quite sure where she fit, and occasionally when she tried to make a joke, it would fall flat because they didn't understand her humor. One such sally came on a day when Marilyn was hours late and as she arrived on the set Paula said: "You can afford to be late, but when you become a big star like Sandra Dee, you'll have to come on time."

Marilyn clearly needed her and depended on her. They would talk about acting, about sense-memory—the idea that she would remember an experience in her life and, having identified with it, translate it into emotion and use it in creating the character in the film. Although Mr. Huston was her director, it was to Paula that Marilyn would look for approval. Fortunately, Huston liked Paula and was always courtly to her.

The night of the party the other members of her entourage came to the house in Virginia City—Allen "Whitey" Snyder; Agnes Flanagan, her hairdresser; Bunny Gardel, her body-makeup lady; Sherlee Strahm, her wardrobe mistress; Rudy Kautzky, her chauffeur; Ralph Roberts, her masseur; and Mae Reis, her secretary. All were members of what she called her "family."

Ralph and Mae would meet with her evenings in her apartment after work. They had a set routine. Ralph Roberts describes it: Marilyn would have a glass of champagne, Mae would have a martini and Ralph a vodka-and-water and they would discuss the day's events. Marilyn loved to watch Mae, whom she nicknamed Maisie, do her imitation of Marlene Dietrich. Mae, a small, dark woman then in her early fifties, would lift her skirt; Marilyn would clap and shout with laughter. "Look at those legs, look at those legs! I wish I had legs like that," she would keep repeating. (At the end of the picture, when we were all leaving for the airport to go to California, I caught the act as Mae, with lifted skirt and one lovely leg extended, was making her entrance into the limousine to join Marilyn, who was doubled up with laughter in the back seat of the car.)

Her "family" cared for her and gave her loyalty and support, but every once in a while she would realize that it was a relationship based on a weekly paycheck and would be concerned lest they became paid courtiers. But they never did. They were fierce in their dedication to her.

Mae Reis was a special friend, who gave her sisterhood and a real sense of familial belonging, but managed to keep her own independence inviolate. She left Marilyn in 1961—perhaps because she felt she could no longer help—but they did keep in touch, and Marilyn made sure that Mae was invited to the President's Ball when she sang her birthday song.

Marilyn cared about Mae and left her $50,000 in her will. When the will was probated there was no money, but some has accrued in the last few years from the films in which she had an interest, and it is good to know that Mae is able to enjoy that windfall now. A discreet, sensitive woman, she has refused all these years to be interviewed about Marilyn. When I went to see her recently, she was kind but definite—she would not talk. Her refusal was eloquent: "I was not an observer—I was part of the whole. It's too painful to remember those moments [apropos of a question I had asked her]. I'm filled with things seen and unseen, done and undone, spoken and untold. I cannot talk. I'm filled with sadness. No matter what people saw on the surface, there was always anxiety and uncertainty." Marilyn's trust was well placed.

They were all there that night—with the exception of Paula and with the addition of Monty. I had come a bit early to check things out, but all was well. From my notes I see that we had guacamole which Marilyn helped prepare with an electric blender, followed by a curry of chicken. All of it was washed down with vintage champagne. There was toasting and laughter, dancing and light talk. Marilyn throughout looked like a little girl—a pleased little girl seated at the middle of a long table in that private dining room with Monty Clift on her right and her "family" all around her.

On Monday we returned to the desert, the wild horses, the wind, the sand and lines to learn. First there were days of tough work with the three male principals when they rode, lassoed, wrestled, threw, trussed and tied up the wild horses. As Gable, Clift and Wallach tried to throw the stallion, Marilyn screamed into the wind, which was high and scattering dust over people and equipment alike: "Stop it; that's not fair!" At this point she has grabbed the rope that Gable is using to tie up the horse. Gable turns (or rather the film character Gay Langland does) and knocks her over, yelling, "Get off me, Roslyn!" She goes off into the desert and screams into the wind, "Murderers!"

This was followed by a scene in which Gable was dragged on the desert floor—it looked in the film as if the wild stallion dragged him. Actually he was attached to a rope from a moving camera car. There has been a great deal of controversy about this sequence. Some journalists after his death claimed that it killed him. What was not generally known was that he had had a previous heart attack, and that he knew exactly how difficult the sequence was and prepared for it. Unlike the neophytes in the film, when he had his wardrobe fittings he insisted upon chaps, shoulder pads, gloves and a sort of all-over corset to be worn underneath. This armor was to protect him from bruises and sand burns, and it did. While the actors were struggling with alkali dust, wind, animals and lines, the representative from the American Society for the Prevention of

Cruelty to Animals stood by to make sure the animals were treated humanely and their strength not overtaxed.

The night before the last day's shooting on location, John Huston gave a joint birthday party for Montgomery Clift and Arthur Miller. Huston had been careful to nudge Marilyn into coming. She arrived with Arthur. It was a small guest list. All of us were relieved that the film was almost finished and we celebrated noisily.

After dinner we went into the bar to shoot craps. When Huston gave Marilyn the dice, she asked: "What should I ask the dice for, John?" His answer: "Don't think, honey, just throw. That's the story of your life. Don't think —do it."

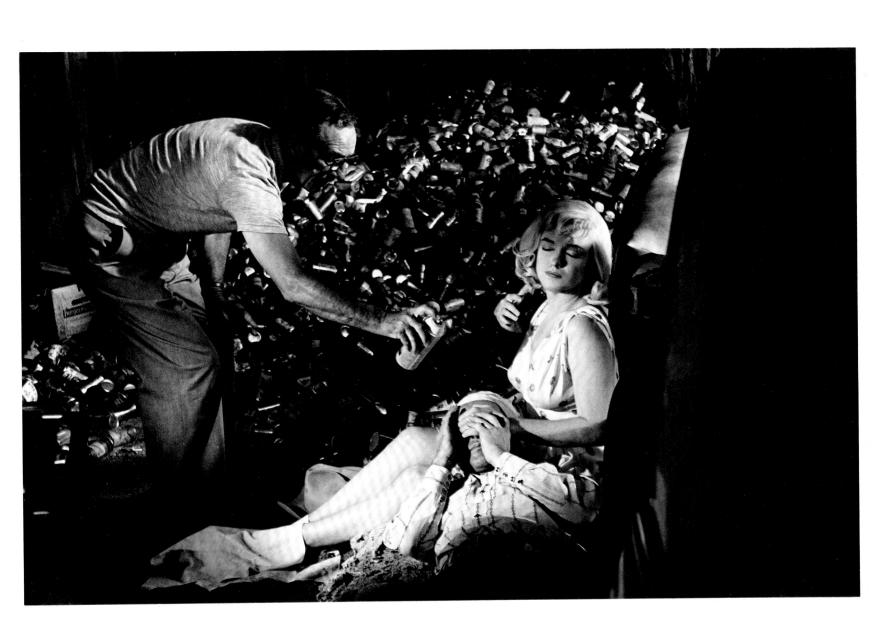

ON LOCATION IN NEVADA DURING THE FILMING OF THE MISFITS.
MARILYN BEING HELD BY HER MAKEUP MAN "WHITEY" (TOP LEFT), BY AN
UNIDENTIFIED MEMBER OF THE CREW (TOP RIGHT) AND BY LEW SMITH, CLARK
GABLE'S DIALOGUE COACH (BOTTOM). FACING PAGE: ELI WALLACH SITS ON HER LAP.

GAMBLING IN RENO, NEVADA. MARILYN HAD THE DICE (TOP).
JOHN HUSTON COACHES HER ON THROWING THE DICE—"DON'T THINK, HONEY,
JUST THROW." FACING PAGE: MARILYN'S REACTION TO A LUCKY TOSS.

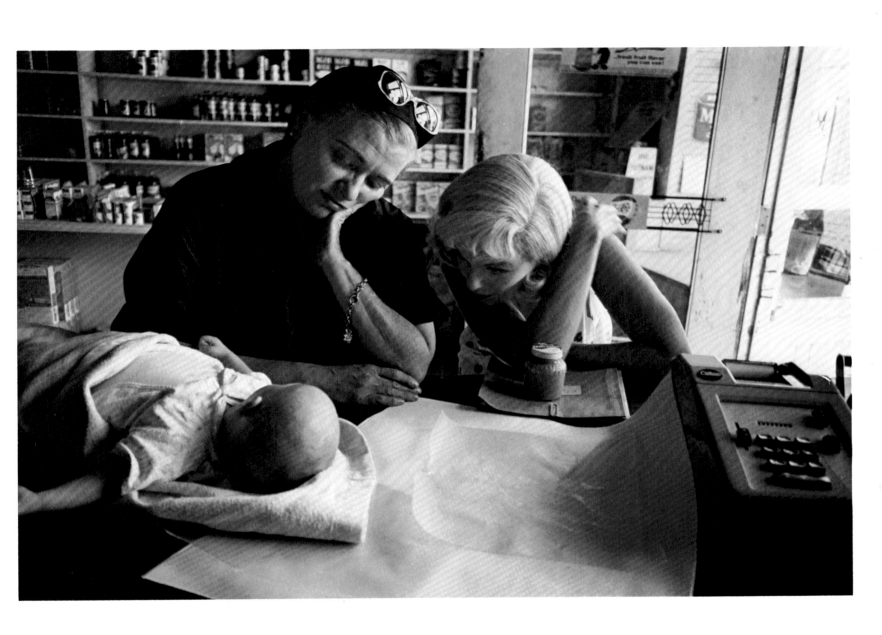

went on to California to arrange a sitting in a studio with Marilyn. (There were ten days of process shooting being done on the soundstage in Los Angeles.) We had amassed acres of documentary shots on location, but what was needed were color portraits for covers for the overwhelming number of requests coming in daily from magazines.

In addition to the Monroe material I was preparing, there was a picture essay on Clark Gable for *Life*. Gable was known as being publicity-shy about his personal life, and when Marilyn heard that he had invited me to come home with him for lunch and a picture session, she was impressed. He told her that although he didn't much trust magazines he did trust me, and that the essay would end with the birth of his child. He said that the reason for his confidence was that *Life* had gotten wind of the fact that his wife had bought a cradle for their child and when the *Life* editor had called me to request a picture of Clark with the empty cradle, I had insisted he not be asked, saying that it was an insensitive thing to do and that he would probably be spooked by the request and refuse. Later, Gable heard about this from the *Life* editor himself.

After her conversation with Clark, Marilyn began to talk about the studio pictures, and when we got to Los Angeles she set a date. I was apprehensive lest she change her mind, but got permission from the studio to use their gallery and to have them provide a "spark" who knew the lighting system. She seemed pleased and talked to Clark about it. Closer to the date, he talked to me when she was around, saying, "This girl has had a long, hard week—make sure she's rested before you start." Marilyn interrupted: "Eve and I have known each other a long time—and she has to do a lot of covers for *Life* and lots of other magazines." Gable said, "Then Eve will understand—I won't allow it until you've had some rest. Do it then." She was delighted by his concern and even more by his sexy grin, so I knew that that sealed it. Now she wouldn't turn back.

And that's the way it went. The time was set for the weekend after she had finished her final scene in the film, and she was only an hour late. The producer had sent a case of champagne and a kilo of caviar, and I had arranged for flowers and Sinatra records.

Whenever we had worked before, it had been haphazard, more or less uncontrolled. Outdoors on Long Island, we had had to depend on the season of the year, the time of day and the sun. At the press conference in New York, we had worked in a crowded room with available house lights for greater verisimilitude. On the junket to Bement, we had had a mix of indoor and outdoor grab.

On *The Misfits*, we had built-in strictures. We worked with the huge klieg lights that were brought onto the desert to fill in the heavy shadows made by the sun; we could only shoot at rehearsals before the "take." (In order to shoot during the "take" it is essential to work with "blimped" cameras to muffle the sound, but these are so heavy as to be stationary, so that the photographer is limited in the image he can make.) Then there's the fact that actors don't like anyone in their "eyeline" when they're working on their roles—it interferes with their concentration. No matter how adroit the photographer is, the limitations are crippling. Occasionally the photographer will ask the actors to rerun a scene for the still camera, but this can only be done after the cinematographer is through, and usually it doesn't work. By the time the actors are finished with the scene, they'll just go through the motions and the result will be wooden. And it's hard to blame them.

But a studio session is an autonomous situation—it provides the greatest chance for control. One can plan one's own lighting, work to one's own time clock, shoot and reshoot, change the subject's hair style, change or add or subtract clothing. Even though there is total freedom, I still dislike studio photography and the contrived images that usually stem from this genre, but Marilyn loved posing and I had learned long ago that to take her on location—the only other way to get the covers done—was to court lunacy. There was practically no way to achieve privacy with Marilyn. She gathered crowds about her the way a magnet gathers metal filings.

Also I was interested in her fantasies about herself. Before we started, I asked, "What do you want to look like? What do you want to be?" "The Botticelli Venus," she said. Remembering the elongated Venus emerging from the shell, I thought she probably meant a Rubens.

On the day, Marilyn brought her "gang"—Agnes Flanagan, Bunny Gardel, Mae Reis, Pat Newcomb, Sherlee Strahm, Rudy Kautzky and "Whitey" Snyder.

When Snyder had laid down the first coat of pancake makeup, she looked around the studio at all the preparations that had been set up for her pleasure and said, "Whitey, remember our first photo session? There was just you and me —but we had hope then."

At this point I motioned to Dick Rowan to start opening bottles of champagne, and we all trooped into the dressing room, entourage and all, to toast her. She saluted us in the mirror with her champagne glass and proceeded to get ready.

These were the days when Jax slacks were fashionable—they were form-fitting trousers that were zipped up the center of the back. Marilyn loved to walk around the dressing room with them unzipped. It was an amusing shot, but I hardly ever got a chance to photograph it because Marilyn would pull the zipper down, I would lift the camera and, almost as if by telepathy, Pat Newcomb—Marilyn's publicist, ever protective of her—would appear, zip it up and disappear. Marilyn would pull the zipper down and the performance with Pat would be repeated. Not a word was said among us, and the game went on.

The make-ready with Marilyn always amused me—particularly the body makeup. Since we were to shoot her in her $300 bikini and her $700 slip, it was necessary to do the full treatment. The makeup is applied like face makeup, with the practitioner shading it from light to dark, and highlighting where needed. It is a time-consuming process, but when Marilyn finally emerged from the dressing room, she was sparkling: hair, face, body, fingernails and toenails all newly attended to. Her entourage applauded.

The only thing to do with this kind of artifice was to camp it up—actually, Marilyn was an early innovator of '50's camp—so the pictures were intended to show this posey side of her. I had ordered blue paper backdrops with floating white clouds which were intended to emphasize the spoof.

Although it had taken three or four hours to prepare her, when we started she worked at speed. We shot color and black-and-white. Her wardrobe mistress had brought not only outfits from the film but some of Marilyn's own clothing, and she changed quickly, her crew speedily doing touch-ups to makeup and hair. The involvement of everyone made for a happy ambience. I remember we laughed a lot, particularly at the end, when I found that although I had had a white paper cone built around us for greater privacy and concentration, the crew had cut eyeholes in the paper and had been watching us all afternoon, supporting her with approving eyes. She had, of course, seen them, and was performing for them, making love to my camera—or really making love to herself—but playing to her public. Being photographed was being caressed and appreciated in a very safe way. She had loved the day and kept repeating that these were the best circumstances under which she had ever worked.

124

ll during the making of *The Misfits*, Marilyn was supposed to have been checking and editing the pictures the Magnum photographers had made. As mentioned earlier, she had the right of refusal on everything, and an elaborate system had been worked out. I quote from James Goode's book: "The fate of the pictures was as follows: the contact sheets showing Monroe went to Eddie Parone [assistant producer] who gave them to Marilyn Monroe who marked out the ones she didn't like with a grease pencil, then gave them back to Harry Mines, *The Misfits* unit publicist, who sent them to Bob Lewin [film-company publicist] who noted all the 'kills.' That is, it was that way last week. It is now changed so that the Magnum sheets go to Allen Snyder, Marilyn's makeup man, who gives them to Harry Mines who sends them to Bob Lewin in Hollywood, who shows them to Rupert Allan, Marilyn's personal publicist in Hollywood."

This House That Jack Built progression was, as anyone could have expected, totally unsatisfactory. With respect, no professional photographer of standing was going to accept being edited by the star's makeup man. It was bad enough when the star did her own editing, but the other arrangement just couldn't work. It was a burden of responsibility that Snyder should not have been expected to shoulder, and at one point when he demurred, Marilyn asked Ralph Roberts, her masseur, to fill in. He refused.

When I returned to New York to consult with Lee Jones, our editor, and check not only my own two hundred sheets of black-and-white contacts and reams of color but those of the other Magnum photographers, we were both distressed. Clearly, the early Marilyn and the later Whitey check marks or "kills" were based on one criterion: that Marilyn look gorgeous. There were whole pages of contact sheets (thirty-six pictures to a sheet) where only one or two pictures would have been passed. With what had been approved, there was no way we could have enough single-picture releases, or have enough material for picture stories.

A visual essay is not just a series of pretty pictures, it is a record of emotion, of situation, of time. Often a lesser picture acts as a conjunction between two better pictures, thus creating a binding entity. There is a visual language with a point of view.

Lee said so many photos had been killed that we didn't have swinging room. The choices, both Marilyn's and Whitey's, were not clever, not even self-serving—all their editing did not display her in the best possible light.

We were indeed in a bind because the film company had decided to release *The Misfits* earlier than planned. Clark Gable had just died, and it was thought that, as a tribute to him, his film should be seen in time for a possible Academy Award. This put the pressure on us to organize our material for release quickly.

Lee and I hit on a plan. We would go to Marilyn, show her the color first, then see if we could enlist her help with the black-and-white material. We would suggest that I sit with her and go through everything that had been done by all the photographers, and thus see if we could put together stories for all the requests. The idea was to ignore the vetoes and start fresh.

On the appointed day, Lee, Edie Capa and I—lugging a projector, everybody's color and cases of black-and-white material—went to Marilyn's apartment on East 57th Street in Manhattan. The street in front of her house was staked out by reporters and photographers keeping vigil. Marilyn had just announced her divorce from Arthur Miller and the vultures were out again.

We first projected all the color we had brought. She loved it, but seemed unwilling to decide which to keep and which to kill. She then called Rupert Allan, her personal publicist, to tell him how much she loved the color.

Lee remembers that through all this there was the sound of a Waring blender whirring away in the background. Marilyn's maid brought in a dish of guacamole (Marilyn had learned to make it from Edith Palmer in Virginia City the night of the party I gave her). Marilyn tasted it before offering it to us. She didn't like the seasoning and disappeared into the kitchen. More whirring noises and she returned with her own blend. With it we drank vermouth, her drink of the week.

According to Lee, she was anxious and perspiring and vacillating about color choices. We meanwhile were trying to get some decisions so we could go on to the important question of how to handle everybody's black-and-white—there was at least twenty times more of that than of color. Lee saw her as putting us through as many hoops as she could get us to jump. I, who knew her better and had had fairly extensive dealings with movie actors, simply took it as what it was—pure Marilyn. She was distracted, wary, as though waiting for a telephone call that never came.

Finally it was decided that I would come next day with two sets of contacts and she and I would go through them all over again—for as long as it took.

It took a full week. Each day I would run the gauntlet of the press waiting outside her apartment house hoping to catch a picture of her. Each day she appeared in her living room bare-footed, silver-toed and wearing her white terry-cloth robe. Each day she would ask the same questions: had the crowd of paparazzi diminished and how come, with everybody outside desperate for pictures, I didn't take any. I explained that my concern was with the thousands we had already taken, and that I wanted to photograph her at some future time on some happier occasion—a new film, a new man…who could guess what surprises might be in store for her?

Daily we set to work, each with a pile of contact sheets, sharpened red grease pencils and a jeweler's loupe for each of us (the pictures on the page measured an inch by an inch and a half and the detail was minute and might need magnification). The first day I explained the problems and the standards appropriate to editing a picture story. She was quick and perceptive, would listen when I explained why a certain picture or situation was necessary, and would concur if she was convinced. If not, we would battle until one or the other backed down.

When she came across a picture of Arthur Miller, she would automatically put an X through it. We would follow the same routine—I would explain that she had no jurisdiction over his pictures but only over any in which she appeared with him. These were a battle. If she could be convinced that a picture was necessary in the context of the story, she would okay it. Otherwise, no. At one point there was a photo of Miller showing her how to do a dance scene in the film. There was no protest over this one. She felt it explained something about the film, and, after all, he had written the script. The ones she balked at were the personal ones that she felt were phony—they had been done at the beginning of the film to throw the press off the true story, which was that their marriage was over.

Whenever she came across a picture with Gable, she would give me meticulous instructions on how to retouch him. The first time she did it, I told her that my kind of photography was "as is," with no tampering. She didn't care for the idea, and persisted in her explicit directions for retouching nonetheless. We both realized that this was her way of thinking she was doing something for him, and I did make the notes she dictated, even though we both knew that nothing would be done.

As the days passed, it was evident that Marilyn was enjoying herself. We would start about noon and go on until five or six o'clock, stopping for a snack or coffee. We worked over a table in her living room. As I remember it, the room was furnished in beiges, a fitting background to her fairness. There was a white grand piano. I also remember two photographs: one of Camus—she had been unhappy over his death and Mae Reis had found a print of him, which she had framed and hung—and a signed photograph of Einstein with a loving inscription to her.

Over the years her biographers have puzzled about how and where she could have met the great scientist and reluctantly concluded that it was just part of the Marilyn legend. According to Eli Wallach, what happened was that when Marilyn and Shelley Winters shared an apartment in Los Angeles, one day they each made up a list of men they would like to have make love to them. Marilyn's list included Albert Einstein. Eli used to tease her about it, so one day she gave him a book of Einstein's letters. On the flyleaf she wrote: "To my dear brother." So Eli gave her a return gift—a picture of Einstein on which Eli wrote "To my darling Marilyn" and signed it "Albert Einstein."

On the day that we finished the editing, I wanted to give Marilyn a gift to show my appreciation, and, recalling that she had once wanted to look like the Botticelli Venus, I stopped at Scribner's on Fifth Avenue and bought her a cahier of Botticelli prints from the Uffizi. I placed the Venus on top of the other prints, wrote on the flyleaf, "To the other Venus," and when we had finished looking at her pictures, I gave her the gift.

She looked at the Venus without recognition, lost, uncertain and appealing, but for what it was hard to tell. It occurred to me that she had created her own Venus, but when the fantasy became the reality, it was too much for her to bear.

ometime in the spring of 1961 Marilyn called me from the hospital in New York where she had undergone surgery for her kidney ailment (the one that had caused her to swell up when we went to Bement, Illinois). She said that *Good Housekeeping* was doing an article on Kenneth, her hairdresser (called Mrs. Kennedy's Kenneth) and that she wanted me to photograph her with Kenneth at her 57th Street apartment the day she came out of the hospital.

She looked fresh and rested, and she and Kenneth played up for the camera, she teasing him about his showing the more photogenic side of his face. We did just one roll of film. It was a simple photo and I did not want to tire her.

Before I left, she reminded me that at our editing sessions we had talked about doing more picture stories on her—how about it? When? I explained that I was now living in London and I would be traveling back and forth between America and Britain. I was under contract to the *Sunday Times* in England and I was sure that my editors and I would come up with some ideas. I'd keep in touch. That was the last time I saw her and the last roll of film that I exposed of her.

On the pavement outside her apartment house there were reporters and photographers. Some of the same faces I had seen at the time of the Miller divorce were there. One of the reporters, recognizing me and desperate for copy, started to interview me: "What was it like to photograph Marilyn?"

I waved him off and went on my way. But the question would not be denied. What was it like to photograph her? It was like watching a print come up in the developer. The latent image was there—it needed just her time and temperature controls to bring it into being. It was a stroboscopic display, and all the photographer had to do was to stop time at any given instant and Marilyn would bring forth a new image.

Lois Smith, who had been her publicist in happier days, was right when she said, "Everything Marilyn was and everything she wanted to be she could just blaze out for the eye of the camera."

She seemed to be blazing out for the press the last two years before her death. She still had the power to engender as much press coverage as she chose—it was just that she and her publicists seemed to have to put more effort into it.

Since the release of *The Misfits* she was on a down with the public. The film was a critical success (the New York *Herald Tribune*: "Here Miss Monroe is magic, not a living pin-up dangled in skin tight satin before our eyes…here is a dramatic, serious, accurate performance.")

Strangely enough, Marilyn does wear the skin-tight $700 satin slip in the film, but apparently this escaped the reviewer. He saw the performance.

The film did not do well at the box office. The day I saw it at a special screening there were titters and what sounded like mocking laughter when her big scene in the desert was projected. When she screamed "Murderers!" at the men who were rounding up the wild horses to be sold for dogfood, what had started out as a slow buzz reached a point of guffaw. It was hard to tell whether it was ridicule or merely nervous reaction.

But, whatever the reaction, it was evident that the audience did not want the new Marilyn—the actress. They did not want her serious, they wanted her to make them laugh, they wanted the sexpot, the comedienne. She was still caught up in the old dilemma that had dogged her career, the dichotomy between being the symbol and being herself, between being the sensual provocation and being the actress. The audience wanted to freeze her in the personality she had created, and she wanted to be free to develop, to grow. She had thought she had won her battle with Hollywood, but now she realized that it had never gone away, just become quiescent.

Marilyn threw herself into trying to regain what she had lost. From this time until her death she tried to enlist all the techniques that had brought her stardom. She went back to the still camera and she permitted more interviews, but this time around she insisted upon seeing the interviews before publication, just as she had insisted upon seeing pictures. She had more confidence now with words. When she talked to Dick Meryman of *Life*, she was articulate and deeply moving. "Fame will go by, and so long, I've had you, Fame. If it goes by, I've always known it was fickle. So at least it's something I've experienced, but that is not where I live."

She battled hard for her right to life as she felt she wanted to live it, but it was still compartmentalized and schizoid if one looks at the way she presented herself at the last. Just as I looked at early pictures of her, I did careful research of the pictures and stories that she frenetically involved herself in at the end. Most of them were published after she died.

There are two sittings with Bert Stern, shot in California for *Vogue*. One is a very elegant, very rich-looking series, in which she poses in black dresses, and the other is a wild, half-nude, almost-out-of-control series in which she poses behind diaphanous scarves.

The fashion sitting, published by *Vogue* after her death, had an elegiac quality about it. The other was published in book form, called *The Last Sitting*. In the book there are contact sheets and color transparencies which Marilyn thought she had "killed" and which she had defaced so they would not be published.

The color originals Bert Stern sent her for approval (he withheld two thirds of them) she felt so strongly about that before she returned them she ripped and mutilated them with a pointed object, probably a hairpin. Speaking of Marilyn's reaction to the pictures, Bert Stern wrote: "She had not only scratched out my pictures, but had scratched out herself." Still, he published them.

When Marilyn went into production for the last film on which she ever worked, *Something's Got to Give*, a remake of a 1940 film, *My Favorite Wife*, she went her old familiar route with her stills. She posed for three photographers simultaneously in a nude swim scene; these were the last pictures she was ever to pose for. She showed nipples and bare bottom and she still managed to appear natural and seemly. She had come full circle. In the beginning was the nude and at the end was the nude. But these were the penultimate pictures.

It is a black paradox, a travesty of all that Marilyn tried so carefully to do with the character she created, to contemplate the last picture that was taken of her. Perhaps it was necessary to photograph her in the morgue, but did it have to be published? To see this abomination is an affront to those of us who knew her and respected her as a woman and a talent, who photographed her with affection and concern, who tried to show her with her foibles and her problems but also with her humor and her warmth and her humanness.

But there is a more fitting epitaph for Marilyn Monroe—the one she made up for herself: "37–22–35." R.I.P.

ACKNOWLEDGMENTS

This book is a loving retrospective. There were no formal interviews, just reminiscences from Marilyn's friends and associates which seemed to form a collective memory of her. It would be hard to say in every case who said what or where one person began or another ended. Our feelings and thoughts about her were circular and mutual. May I thank all who participated?: Sandy and Lou Achitoff, Angela Allen, Drusilla Beyfus, Edith Capa, Elliott Erwitt, Stanley Flink, Elizabeth Gallin, Burt Glinn, Ernst Haas, Yvonne Halsman, James Haspiel, Frieda Hull, John Huston, Lee Jones, George and Cass Levine, Roddy McDowell, Inge Morath, Edward Parone, Tom Prideaux, Mae Reis, Ralph Roberts, Norman Rosten, Jeanne Sakol, Lois Smith, John Springer, Frank Taylor, Eli Wallach and William Wetherby.

Gratitude to Lin Smith and Deborah Weinreb for the enormous amount of work involved in typing and in ordering prints, and for the general dogsbody effort that goes into getting a picture book ready for the editor's eyes; and to Robin Bell, who made the prints.

Special thanks to Martha Kaplan, Mary Maguire, Ellen McNeilly and Robert Scudellari at Knopf for consideration and help beyond expectation; and to friends and family who lent support beyond the call of friendship: Francis Arnold, Michael Arnold, Dora Charkow, Jack and Gertrude Cohen, Lucy Kroll, Charles and Diana Michener, Marcia Panama, Ann Quinn, Michael Rand, Sherley Roland, Carol Ryan and Charlotte Walsh.

And to Robert Gottlieb, whom I cherish as friend, editor and publisher.

GRAPHIC NOTE

THE TEXT OF THIS BOOK WAS SET IN A FILM VERSION OF BASKERVILLE.
BASKERVILLE IS A FACSIMILE CUTTING FROM TYPE CAST FROM THE ORIGINAL MATRICES OF A
FACE DESIGNED BY JOHN BASKERVILLE. THE ORIGINAL FACE WAS THE
FORERUNNER OF THE MODERN GROUP OF TYPE FACES.

COMPOSED BY TYPOGRAPHIC IMAGES, INC., NEW YORK, NEW YORK.
COLOR REPRODUCTIONS SEPARATED BY NORTHWESTERN COLORGRAPHICS, INC., MENASHA, WISCONSIN.
COLOR REPRODUCTIONS AND TWO-COLOR STONETONE REPRODUCTIONS PRINTED
BY RAPOPORT PRINTING CORPORATION, NEW YORK, NEW YORK.
BOUND BY A. HOROWITZ AND SONS, FAIRFIELD, NEW JERSEY.
PRODUCTION AND MANUFACTURING DIRECTED BY ELLEN MCNEILLY.
GRAPHIC ARTS DIRECTED BY R.D. SCUDELLARI.